D1707048

Authentic

Actualization

Strive for Revelation
Land on Inspiration
       -Andy Swaithes, PhD

Don't take yourself too seriously,
no one else does! :)
    -Andy Swaithes, PhD

Authentic Actualization

Change your view, then change your vision

Andy Swaithes, PhD

Authentic Actualization

ISBN 9798785961531

@crackerjackprofessor

Dedication

This book is dedicated to my wife and children, hopefully I don't embarrass them with my opinions on helping humanity. :)

Algorithmic Authenticity

This book is the result of a time in my life filled with great confusion. Being firmly rooted now in my '40s, entering the Fall of my life and also being on the downswing, I would have assumed I would have had a lot less questions and I would have more clarity in my life. When in actuality it has been quite the opposite. With my needs being met and a successful attempt at not being as busy, I find myself with more and more time to be with myself.

Topically, this may sound like paradise with some people, having a cushy work from home schedule, where you don't have to go grocery shopping during peak hours and you have the flexibility to work with your kids' schedules. Ironically, I now find that I have more time for self-care, which in turn creates a stronger need for more self-care. I have realized that my goals, ambitions and aspirations have all led to a highly unsatisfying professional life. Many of the long-term goals I have set, are nowhere near coming to fruition and I feel as though I have been living someone else's career.

There is a section later in the book that talks about people just passing through your emotional playground. They think that they want to be there, but ultimately, they are just there for the ride and they will be moving on soon. Through my research and teachings, I have unveiled the fact that I suffer from a great deal of cognitive dissonance in my own life and I feel strongly urged to make some changes.

Therein lies the rub, right! How in the world do you take a career in corporate America and suddenly scrub it for a life of service, teaching, coaching, ministering and ultimately charitable activities? I can tell you that if I ever figure it out I will let you know (and I hope you will reciprocate), however what I do know is that I know the path put in front of me, vs. the one behind me, is far more authentic. The hyper-awareness I have absorbed from teaching from this text at multiple institutions and multiple classes, has allowed and afforded me with the blessings/curses of active introspection.

The blessings of intentional reflection are completely real and unavoidable. I know that in order for me to be transparent and real, I must listen to the promptings I am feeling in regards to taking a new path in my career. The curse is the timeframe and urgency. The headspace created by this previously mummified authenticity is next to impossible to shake off. It follows me around like a stray animal and is as demanding as an infant! I was guilty of **authenticity debt**, as every time I was trying to be authentic

I weakened and I withdrew. True resilience is tough and things like heartbreak and true loss are impossible to manufacture.

Utilizing Maslow's Hierarchy of needs and coupling that with authenticity, has shown me my own path and delivers the most **Authentic Actualization** while leveling up the needs ladder. During this journey, we will stumble upon extremely valuable tools like clarity, discernment and awareness; to better understand our true selves and peeling back the layers to show the world how we are in fact unique. Please don't discount when these tools show up as it may be in an unconventional setting and could also scare the shit out of you. **By itself, <u>awareness</u> could be your most valuable weapon in the fight to be authentic.**

I have felt impressed upon, that the tips/suggestions in this book will have a similar impact on those who read. Again, that can be good or bad, it just depends on how much value you place on my help. *I just hope the information presented here will allow you to have the same type of breakthroughs that I have had and also allow you the courage to* **sacrifice the ideal, for a true sense of the real.**

To have the life you presently don't,
You have to do what others won't

Maslow's Hierarchy of Needs

Contents

15

Stop Suffering from memory and imagination, There is literally nowhere else you can be, but here right now!

Introduction

Since the pandemic began back in March of 2020, the years since have been filled with opportunities, challenges and priority shifts. In fact, I thought that the worst of it was behind me when 2021 began. **In actuality it was the year of the Country Western Song. You know how it goes, I lost my ….. (fill in the blank)!** Along the way, my wife and I have created a habit that includes an evening walk that includes taking the time to have deep conversations or discuss important topics that affect our community as well as our immediate universe.

With my PhD in Psychology, experience in performance coaching, knowledge of human behavior and motivations, I started putting down ideas on paper on how to best help ourselves as well as loved ones. Said ideas were soon organized and shortly after, morphed into what follows.

These writings act as a hybrid between a self-help and a how-to manual. With luck, the content in this book will not only help answer some questions about motivation, but will also inspire you to problem solve and find new solutions to unresolved challenges in your life.

When I think about the adversity that this pandemic has provided, I go back to an inspiring quote about the mythical Phoenix and its strife, failure and moxie. A quote from Richard Alois states,

"The Phoenix is always consistent as an awesome being that is large in structure and wingspan. It undergoes differentiated versions of destruction, rebirth, and renewal. The consistent parallelism is that the Phoenix is always the symbol of undying perseverance, in spite of the expected opposition and blockade towards its goals. It goes on, gallant and confident. Unwavering in its struggle towards the accomplishment of its mission. The continued fight for success, the Phoenix emerges from the ashes, a new bird, better than its old self. The new reincarnated self is better equipped to pursue its mission again. This cycle of renewal, death and destruction goes on and on."

I often use this quote as a starting block in order to embrace the frequency of trials in my life, find the path forward and expect that challenges will continue to occur! The understanding of where we are as humans from a motivational perspective comes from a deep understanding of the linear path that we must follow in order to be our best selves. This has never been more apparent to me as to when I gave up my substance abuse and was able to steadily climb the ladder of needs as described by Abraham Maslow in his book "A Theory of Human Motivation". I had read his theories earlier in my time in academics, but when looking at the practical application of growth and perseverance, it has now become very clear how important this theory is.

With that being said, I feel that a thorough and in-depth understanding of human motivation is necessary not only to help my individual situation, but to help anyone who is asking questions about growth, ambition and success. The chapters of this book provide a precise path of boxes to check in order to become our best selves, reach our potential and dissolve obstacles. Also, it helps to literally and figuratively be on the same page with changing the approach to finding joy and happiness.

The intention of this book is not to invalidate individuals who have mental health issues or disorders. With a psychology background, I completely understand that chemical imbalances and/or trauma cannot be cured with my ideas and concepts. My intention is to take high functioning adults with solid emotional baselines and help them with understanding the mental process behind motivation and growth in order to change their outlook and vision.

This text is filled with real life applications, accompanied by minimal theoretical suggestions and data that tend to sometimes act as filler. It is intended to be an evidence-based performance manual to help answer questions about where potential breakdowns occur and guidance on how to persevere.

Keep in mind that as you go through the sections of this book, please understand that all the strategies and suggestions are remedies that work in multiple facets, and are transferable to any growth opportunity presented. Also, keep this saying top of mind as you read the text:

Authenticity vs. Responsibility

My objective for this writing is to have good flow and to provide a tool that could theoretically be read in one sitting. **I am <u>not</u> all things to all people, however being an academic, I am looking to help individuals by providing fun-sized experiential context in order to help create sustainable prosperity, which empowers individuals to find their own authentic positive change spark.**

Chapter 1

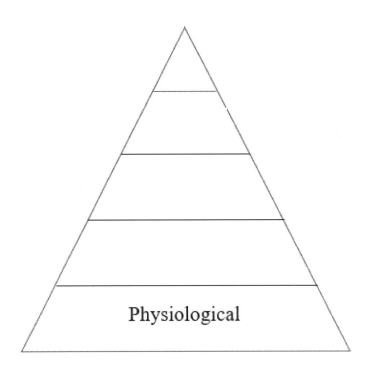

Basic human needs start with having enough food, water and shelter in order to function throughout the day. Having enough of these things in current supply, in order to not worry about them, is the key to having this need met. It is also important to get enough sleep and live in an area with clean air to breathe and water to drink. But what else is there to consider when looking at these basic human needs? How in this day and age has our society maximized and possibly exploited this, with taking it a bit too far? In the sections below, we will look at some issues that arise from the ability to not only have this need met, but having some take it too far and looking at additional potential that can come from a deeper understanding of the most basic of needs.

- **Consumption**
- **Dynamic Movement**
- **Addiction**
- **Stress**
- **Spirituality**

The chapter begins by taking an alternative approach to diet and looks to tie in psychological attributes in order to maximize our ability to regulate what we consume. We will then move on to the benefits of active meditation provided by exercise and how it can enhance creativity and critical thinking. After we discuss the value of movement and physical activity, this chapter will discuss how addictions form with the accompaniment of triggers and how these addictions can limit your ability to focus on desired tasks. We will discuss an action plan to reduce addictions as well as provide rationale for a clear vision into how to take your life back! After addiction, the chapter will lead us to discuss stress and further understand the negative implications stress has on our decision making and creative thinking abilities. And lastly, we will discuss the value of spirituality and why it is a physiological need. Whether you are a religious person or secular humanist, we will dive deeper into the desire to be a good person, help others and seek worthiness.

(Bio)Logical Beginnings

"You don't have a soul.
You are a soul.
You have a body."
C.S. Lewis

Consumption:

In its simplest form "consumption", means to devour or absorb. Now I could start this chapter stating that you need to rid yourselves of all unnecessary foods such as soda, candy, pastries etc. and simply eat to survive as early humans did, by hunting and gathering. But I won't start there. I will start with a realistic approach to what we put in our bodies in order to fuel our lives. I am not a nutritionist or a dietician, but I feel as I can speak to the psychology of eating and why we experience daily cognitive dissonance with what we ingest. We all know that some foods are not healthy and possibly even bad for us, yet we partake in behaviors far too often that worsen our health.

Right here and now I am sitting in my office after I got done with a 6-mile run, feasting on candy, soda and orange sherbet. I feel like I deserve this reward after exerting myself on a moderately severe workout. Then only to need another workout tomorrow to burn off the empty calories I just consumed! Where does this cycle end? In fact, the second biggest motivator I have to exercise (the first is to live as long as possible), is to ease my mind into acceptance of the formula of calories coming in must equal or be less than calories burned. Although flawed, my rationale is that if I run a specific amount of distance, I can have a specific amount of junk food.

The reality of our world is that life is difficult, unpredictable and more times than not we just need a little help with getting to the next level. That help can come in the form of an energy drink or a candy bar. Most of us who struggle with consumption, focus on just getting from checkpoint to checkpoint with no real plan of attack or understanding of how to fix it.

This time last year, I was 265 pounds and was living the ideal unhealthy lifestyle. Shoveling in as much caffeine, starch and sugar as (literally) humanly possible just trying to survive. With a high stress job and a new boss, I was trying to make a name for myself by being uber available and glued to my computer screen. There was no way I was going to allow myself any kind of real behavioral change as I was doing what I thought was right. Providing for my family was my main objective and my health was secondary.

This was obviously not a conscious thought, as I was just caught up in the hustle and bustle of Corporate America and didn't take the time to better understand why it was that way. It is a lot like the analogy of boiling the frog. If you throw a frog in a boiling pot of water it jumps out, however if you put the frog in the water and gradually increase the heat the frog will die. That is where I was a year ago, I was boiling to death. I had gone from 170 pounds when I met my wife, to 95 pounds heavier after 15 years of marriage. Like the frog, I didn't even realize the changes that had taken place.

My wife had suggested that we take a vacation to celebrate not only our anniversary, but to incorporate our honeymoon as we were unable to financially take one at the time we were married. I looked in the mirror and had a conversation with myself, looking for a plan to drop more weight than I ever had. How was I to do this? I want my junk food, I want my sweets, it is a part of my routine and honestly part of my identity! I looked (again) at the latest diet crazes. Nice, I thought, I can go down the no carb diet again and have the same lousy results as I did a few years back. I can only eat vegetables for a few months (despite only lasting 4 hours) and see what that does for me. I can even try this crazy thing of only eating things without a face. Really! How in the world is this going to make sense for me?

I needed to get into my brain and understand what may work for me. Mind over Fatter, right? Keep in mind this is tricky, (we will discuss this further in later chapters) as the brain automatically rejects change. It thinks, "Hey, I am alive so why would I change?". *In life, if things appear to be socially, psychologically,* *physiologically or emotionally hard, they are more than likely RIGHT.* **Make sure to circle back on this statement as you try and affect some positive change in your life.**

So, I took a look at what has worked in other avenues of my life. Was I better at adding things or taking them away? Was I better at introducing more structure to my activities or reducing constraints? It was time to take a long hard look at my overall behaviors and apply that to how to make a difference in my diet.

I looked at my personal life and started to understand that despite liking to fly by the seat of my pants, I preferred my wife letting me know in advance our families schedule and when/where I was expected to be. I also looked at my work and realized that I was a much better decision maker in the morning than I was in the afternoon and extrapolating that to assume that I could be more disciplined in the morning. I am also a bit stubborn and needed to have control over how this was going to take place.

There is a running joke in my house that I seldom let others tell me what to do and that I make my own version of macaroni and cheese, as the back of the box **isn't** going to tell me how to make dinner! Finally, I looked at my relationship with my teenage daughter; as we have an agreement that no matter how much sense plans make, we don't do anything spur of the moment. If she comes to me at 4pm and says that her friends just asked her to go to the movies at 430pm, but her chores/homework aren't done, she is not able to go. We don't make impulsive decisions and we surely don't respond to the fear of missing out.

With my behaviors being slightly dissected, I began to put into place a dietary schedule that may be favorable to what could work for me. The key words there are that it **could** work for **me**. No guarantees and no easy path. Almost immediately I decided to pursue intermittent fasting. In my life I tend to respond well to urgency and deadlines. If I tell myself to stop eating by a specific time, I will have an automatic stopwatch in my mind where nothing shall be consumed after a specific time. Moreover, I am not recommending a fasting program for anyone, I am simply relaying my story in hopes of helping others to find a path to success.

I also remembered a story my grandmother had told me about how during the Great Depression, families would feed their children as often as they could, but wasn't necessarily every day let alone 3 times per. The parents and grandparents would eat only on Sundays. WOW, I remember thinking, "They would only eat once a week?" That was obviously shocking as it is so foreign to me.

I had a similar conversation with my dad about his upbringing in Colorado, and how his parents could only afford to eat on alternating nights. Ultimately, they would take turns as they had 9 children to feed. At that point I knew some sort of fasting was possible and I began to give it a try. The stories of my relatives are certainly not ideal, however it helped me realize that I was consuming more than what my body needed in order to survive. As a math guy, I thought to myself, if I consume 600 calories at every meal and goodness knows how many snacks, there must be a way to lose weight simply by setting a cutoff during the day.

Initially, I wanted to do one thing at a time. Of course, it would be great to completely change the time I eat, what I eat and introduce a strict and strenuous exercise regimen, however I didn't feel that to be realistic. First, I was going to experiment to find out if I could handle only eating between the hours of 6am and noon, seven days a week. With my weight being so high I felt as though I couldn't afford to gain anymore and was even concerned about what would happen if I maintained.

I had discussed how this new eating schedule would work with my family as I needed complete buy in and support. If I were to go down this path, I would no longer be able to have family dinners and would ultimately be eating on my own for the foreseeable future. Every member of my family understood and I was on my way to weight loss. As I mentioned earlier, I was not changing anything about my diet except when I would be eating. I still have junk food in my refrigerator in my office and cold soda inches away from my workspace. This new way of living began in October and I was giving myself until the beginning of March before I needed to see significant improvement, as that was when we were taking our vacation.

The first week was obviously excruciating as not only did I have hunger pains almost every evening, I was also not seeing much success on the scale. In fact, I had lost a few pounds in the first few days, but almost none in the second week! How in the world is this possible and not to mention, why the hell am I doing this to myself? All of these thoughts flooded my mind on a daily basis, but I was still determined to see it through until March.

I began to time it perfectly, as I would wake up at 5:45am and prepare the meal that would break my fast. The issue that I saw early on (now that I am looking back), is that I was limiting myself to just breakfast foods that I was never really fond of in the first place. I was limiting myself to different types of eggs with different condiments to vary the taste. I would go from salsa to ketchup to wing sauce, then back around. This was getting old fast, but I was still determined to lose the weight and that I could make this work.

A trick that I learned during week 3 is that if I really wanted ice cream or a cheeseburger, I would prepare myself to eat it first thing when I woke up. If at night the family was watching a movie with candy and popcorn and I really wanted it, I would have it first thing the next morning! No more breakfast food rotations, as I was incorporating more of what I liked and more foods that satisfied my cravings. Along this path I also realized that I couldn't eat out as much as most places that I frequented didn't open until 11am. With that in mind, it is considerably difficult to get to a restaurant, put your name down, be seated, order and eat all before noon.

I was getting really good at planning my meals and preparing them first thing in the morning. I would get my fill and if I needed a snack about 30 minutes before the fast would stop, I scheduled an alarm to go off as a reminder to shovel as many cookies, chips or candy in my mouth as I could before the stopwatch went off at noon. This schedule was proving itself and I was losing weight at a healthy yet exciting clip. The fact that I could incorporate what was working for me behaviorally in other aspects of my life, really helped me to conquer this goal as well.

With a few weeks to go before the vacation I realized that I had lost 35 pounds and was looking and feeling better than I had in years! I was able to be more active with my family, I was able to climb up the stairs in my house without feeling like I was having a heart attack and other things in my body started working like they did when I was in my 20s. I was now more regular and my libido was restored! This experiment had worked out better than I had planned and I realized that if this type of food schedule was working for me, then who else may it work for and what are the limits to this type of thinking?

It is not just the scheduling that did the trick, it was the investigation about what works for me. I didn't change what I ate, however I have a deep interest in nutrition and anticipate at some point making subtle and sustainable adjustments. Right now, I think I will be miserable without eating the things that make me happy, despite knowing that it is food that tastes good, but doesn't make me feel good. I am fully aware that caffeine, trans fats and fast food are not ideal, yet I am strictly focusing on what works for ME. It's all about keeping an up to date and real account of what is top of mind from an intake perspective.

According to Darin Olien, he states in his book, "Superlife" that if you open a bag of Doritos, the overpowering perfume of salt, sugar and fat, is designed to trick you into thinking you are eating something essential. This psychological aspect has certainly reeled me in; however, I am aware of it and plan to eventually make adjustments.

Ultimately, you know your body better than anyone else and I have a feeling that you have tried multiple diets over the span of your life. It is now time to circle the wagons and take things that work from multiple theories to compile what works. If you couple a few ideas from what you know works and incorporate that with behaviors from other aspects of your life, I know you can achieve the success I have, by making a few realistic and proven behavioral adjustments.

Once I returned from my vacation with my wife, I took my weight loss to another level as I incorporated exercise into my daily routine, as I am convinced about the positive physiological and psychological effects of exercising.

Dynamic Movement:

Life in the twenty-first century is filled with convenience and innovation. Activities that previously required active pursuit have now been simplified, as no longer do we need to go out and hunt for our food or chop down wood for heat. All of these modern luxuries have indirectly limited our physical activity and unless we are aware of the fact that we don't get as much exercise as our ancestors we are not going to bring it back to our routines. If you look back to the previous section, I discussed how I had lost 35 pounds by taking a look at my eating habits and incorporating the psychology of what works for me in other aspects of my life. When I started losing weight, I was too fat and out of shape to even work out. I couldn't do any exercising that didn't cause me pain or discomfort.

When I returned home from my vacation with my wife in March, after 3 months of intermittent fasting, I was finally ready to bring exercise into the fold. I was ready to start accepting the invitations from my friends to play golf and tennis, and was ready to start running again, which I had loved in my twenties. During the course of most of my thirties, I was focused on providing and being a husband and father. Exercising was secondary to my real responsibilities and after all, the metabolism of a younger man is pretty forgiving. But with every year older, things recover a bit more slowly.

Also, a main contributor to my laziness is that I was tied to a computer and it seemed like I sat down at a desk more than I slept! Putting exercise on the back burner was one of the biggest mistakes I could have made as I was continually seeking to make a name for myself with creating best practices and efficiencies within my sales territories, but in actuality I was beating my head against the wall using the same recycled ideas that have been floating around sales professionals for years. What I needed was to be original and cutting edge, and the work schedule that I was accustomed to, was not producing such results.

What I have found over the past 6 months is that not only does exercise get your heart rate up and helps you to lose weight, but there are also significant psychological benefits to creating a regular exercise schedule. This process started as a way to look better for a vacation and has continued to build along the way. Initially it was just a change in behavioral eating patterns, and once I plateaued there, I felt that I was ready to take the next step with running around my neighborhood a few miles at a time to take my weight loss to the next level.

Over the first few weeks of exercising the weight fell off at an exciting yet concerning rate. I began to feel like a superhero as every day the scale would go lower and my running distance would go up. This was the perfect perpetuation of health, and I couldn't be happier. My motivation was high, I was seeing firsthand and in real time the fruits of my labor and I yearned for the next challenge.

Before I began to really build my routine, I knew and was aware of the effects of dopamine and how valuable it was to our overall happiness. I knew that it helped us to feel happy, but that was the extent of my knowledge. There was no way for me to comprehend the short- and long-term effects of dopamine releases and how I would yearn for that feeling that was felt during exercise, more so than how I would yearn to see the scale every morning or to track how many miles I ran on any given day/week/month.

Exercise is a great way for you to get back to the fact that physical health matters and that homeostasis is a fundamental need that must be achieved/maintained in order to continue to climb the ladder that eventually leads to growth. What I have found with the awareness of how I feel with increased sustained levels of dopamine, are that I am in a much better mood, my attention levels are heightened, and I am far more creative now than I ever have been.

In fact, the reason for me to write this book came to me during a run and I was able to create the outline and subsets over the course of a week. I felt like being active really allowed me to manufacture and curate ideas and not solely be creative. I have been able to use the time on my run to problem solve and look at situations in a different light in order to use somewhat fresh eyes and not take similar and unsuccessful approaches.

Another perk about exercising, more specifically running, is the ability to focus on the simple task of being in the moment and pushing your body to achieve your workout. Whether you are training for a race or doing CrossFit, it is impossible to push your body to complete a physical task while simultaneously trying to multitask. Slowing our brains down to focus on the moment has been all over literature and has worked its way into mainstream. **Simple tasking** does have its advantages as it provides clear direction and intention. How many of us would love to have at least an hour a day of clear thought that gave us a break from the hustle and bustle of normality?

This is an **unconventional form of meditation**, as we typically associate stillness with dark rooms and quiet noises. While trail running, it is very difficult to focus on anything but the rock in front of you or not stepping on a rattlesnake. This **active introspection** was an unexpected benefit to an already advantageous activity. Ironically, you are able to kill two birds with one task, it is just a bit unexpected. Active introspection is even more present when we push our physical bodies to the limit. During difficult Yoga classes, the majority of the class is spent on building strength and flexibility, but at the end, we are rewarded with savasana, whereas you are able to lie down and be at one with your thoughts and recover. During this time, we experience hyper-active introspection. **We are never more in tune with our bodies than when we are experiencing discomfort!**

In order to see true change, you must have a better relationship with your body as through the sweat comes connection!

During active introspection, you are finally allowing your **subconscious** to return from the vacation you put it on during your constant barrage of social media concentration, which allows true creativity and inspiration to break through. I think about Moses, Jesus and Buddha and how they spend time alone whilst in the wilderness and had profound insight. There is value in these types of activities and if you can connect meditation to physical activity, the sub-conscious will do the heavy lifting, as it pertains to problem solving, imagination and critical thinking.

Strive for Revelation, Land on Inspiration

At the time this book was written I had lost 65 pounds and I was able to keep the routine that I had put in place months before. **The ability to sustain this behavior was due to the psychological benefits I saw through the transition of going from fat to fit. The reason for keeping the habits in place are not vain or singular, but hardwired into my psychology of being. This is how real change is achieved, it cannot be for topical or superficial reasons. Finding a place for the knife-edge between the fight or flight response during physical activity creates immersion and practice needed to transfer to the other avenues of your life. Calm and stability is promoted here in difficult situations or conversations.**

If you want to make a change, look deeper into what moves and pushes you. At that point you will have a real gage for change!

Addiction:

In the introduction, I mentioned that I had given up drinking when I was 33 and it is the best decision I have ever made. It propelled me into a world of clarity and better decision making. There is a common misconception about addiction, as highly functioning addicts aren't homeless under the freeway. There are a lot of people out there that could be a little better at a lot of things if they were to give up some/lessen the intake of substances.

In this section we are going to discuss the struggles that are associated with addictions and how to see the light. The thing about addiction that I realized a long time ago, is that it's not what you are addicted to. There are many addictions out there in the ever-changing and complicated world, but despite having an addiction to food or pornography or exercise, the true fact of the matter is that the afflicted are really addicted to, or **crave being conscious**.

The unique thing about addictions is that it forces you to be conscious and in the moment. Depression and regret live in the past while anxiety and panic live in the future. Let's look at a food addiction (as you can substitute with any other addictions if needed) and try to understand the psychology behind why people overeat. A situation can manifest itself to fill your evening with anxiety and the only thing you can think about is getting fast food and getting your fill in order to forget about the issues at hand. While we are in the act of eating, nothing else matters. The outside world ceases to exist and your entire universe consists of the act of eating, I call this **dirty consciousness**. There is no worry that your issue with a coworker could lead to punitive measures. There is no anxiety that your job could be cut, due to a down economy. All that matters is you and your food.

The way that this becomes an issue is if we have craving for more and more consciousness. **If you are conditioned for food (addiction) to be your buffer than you will seek it out more and more.** Back before I stopped drinking, I used to drive around town for a living and sell adult beverages to chain stores. The days were long and I felt that I could do better and that I needed to move on. I was applying to multiple positions outside of the industry; however, I was not getting any responses back. Every day on my way home from work, I would stop by a bar with coworkers and have a few beers in order to blow off steam.

It wasn't that I was going through withdrawals and absolutely needed to intake water brewed with hops and barley, what I really needed was to take some time away from my reality and just focus on the act of drinking the beer or being in the moment. Consciousness was my addiction, and I did all I could to reconcile what I thought was out of my control.

These behaviors become routine and before you know it you crave these behaviors and you become dependent on how they make you feel. Despite the issues of dependency, another issue with these types of **cravings** is that they **suffocate** what is important to you and don't let you grow. Not until you can be aware of your surroundings enough to put a stop to what is bringing you down, does the healing process begin.

At 33, I stopped drinking cold turkey. I knew that at that point in my life too many intentions and behaviors were spent circulating around how comfortable I felt with a beer in my hand. I can remember the last beer that I had at dinner with my wife on May 27, 2012. I use this as a reminder of the fact that I was able to control the outcome and my ability to walk away from a habit that had been my shadow for far too long.

I knew that my craving for drinking was suffocating my ability to pursue any and all of my goals, as it was always front and center. I had things that I wanted to accomplish and I knew that my drinking was suffocating all my hopes and dreams and it needed to stop. My whole life I knew that I wanted to play the guitar. In fact, I got my first guitar for Christmas when I was 15. I had carried it around with me throughout my adult life. Why in the world had I never taken an official lesson and why wasn't I even able to tune it? It becomes more and more difficult to be in the right mindset to learn and instrument or take on a monumental task while drinking or hungover. This craving was killing my ambition and holding me back!

I knew that if I was able to make the choice to stop allowing drinking to suffocate my dreams of: buying a home, going to get my PhD, helping my family reach their potential, that I was going to be a force for good. Once I made the choice and communicated the goal with my wife there was no looking back. Despite it being one of the best decisions I had made, it wasn't exactly the easiest of paths.

With great change comes a high level of reinvention, that took some time to get used to. I was in a career that dealt with social gatherings with customers and friendships I had, which highly involved drinking. I had to learn how to be comfortable with myself as there was no way to flee the reality of the event by craving the consciousness that drinking provided. I needed to be strong and this is where the reprioritization of my goals came in, that I was finally to be rid of the suffocation of my craving. It is certainly a vicious circle, however with the awareness of what is holding you back, it is certainly attainable.

Something else that occurred that took me by surprise is that once I stopped drinking, I simply transitioned to another addiction, soda and food. I certainly understand that these are better than drinking, with far less cognitive ramifications, however I was substituting one for another. This is where the incremental weight gain came in and despite taking a few years for the frog to boil, I finally reached maximum density in December 2019.

The awareness of addiction came to fruition as I realized that I was simply transplanting one addiction for another, so make sure you are on the lookout for this. Once you have the awareness of your shortfalls and what changes you need to make, try to substitute bad cravings for beneficial ones. Try to replace dirty consciousness with meditative exercise (**clean consciousness**). They both produce the same ability to be present, but the clean versions help to break through your ceiling. The goal of transitioning away from addiction is to try and be a little bit better at a lot of things.

There are a few topics touched on here that we will cover more in Chapter 5. First, goal reorganization is crucial to reframing growth and self-actualization. There must be a focused effort to truly find out what is holding you back and the assertion to alienate your cravings to create positive change. Willpower is not the answer, as ultimately you are fighting yourself and guess what? You lose every time!

Second as we look at the psychology behind addiction, we must know that to make sustainable change we cannot attack the actions alone. If an alcoholic has tried to stop drinking multiple times over their adult life, we must look deeper than their desire to stop cold turkey. Our thoughts lead to our feelings, which lead to our behaviors (continued in Feelings Forecast, Chapter 5). There must be a change with our thoughts to eventually change our behaviors. Take for example a prognosis of liver failure for the same individual, who now has to find a donor or has limited time left. Their outlook (thoughts) have drastically changed, thus affecting how they feel about their scenario, which will more than likely lead to changed behaviors. This is one example and one addiction. Use this insight to help with your own unique struggles.

Stress:

At first glance, when I think of stress, I think of things happening out of my control or situational surprise. It is viewed as the degree of which pressures influence coping levels. Stress used to be something that I had to deal with that was more of an inconvenience or a deterrent than anything else. In my life I have realized that there are clean types of stress and dirty types of stress and your viewpoint makes all the difference. **Dirty stress (distress)** is crippling and has been known to cause all kinds of mental and physical ailments. But what if there was a way to change (reframe) how we perceive stress and turn it into something advantageous?

We will discuss this more in Chapter 5 (Feelings Forecast) when we further discuss the thought model, but when we look deeper at dirty and **clean stress (eustress),** we must understand the chemical release that accompanies both. Clean stress that comes from identifying stress as a challenge releases dopamine and serotonin that helps us to be more creative and better problem solvers. When we think of crippling or even debilitating stress (dirty), cortisol and epinephrine (adrenaline) are released from the adrenals and promotes critical and intolerant behaviors which has a serious impact on being creative. Discussed in the thought model, we will look at how thoughts lead to feelings. **This couldn't be clearer, as when the chemical reactions come from our thoughts can be clean or dirty, leading to clean/dirty feelings. We can literally be in control of our homeostasis (what chemicals are released) through controlling our thoughts.** I call these situations **stress showdowns**, as when we are faced with a difficult situation, and we are unsure what we should do. It is all about how we process the information.

Taking a situation like, "I am overwhelmed about all the work I have to do before I can go on vacation", can be cleaned to now resemble, "I have time to complete what I need to before my vacation" or "I understand completely what is expected of me before I leave work". It is all how you view your reality. In Chapter 5, we will go into a few more examples and I will provide a diagram to work with, in order to help with cleaning stress in the future. This way of thinking is exampled throughout this book and can be used in many forms of challenges throughout your life. Use it freely!

Once clean stress is present, the potential is limitless. As the awareness of clean stress provides direction and motivation to feel accomplishment and focus on what is important to us. Cleaning our stress allows us to feel good about ourselves, develop higher esteem and allows us a clearer vision in order to prevail in future stress showdowns.

Another way stress showdowns enter my world is with decision making. By no means am I indecisive, however I want to make sure that I am calculated and ultimately end up making the correct decision. Being a responsible and pragmatic adult, I have come to the realization that I cannot have it all and in order to have as much clean stress as possible, I set up certain parameters that favor success.

First, **I view most difficult choices as dichotomous and state the simple fact of, "would I rather sacrifice now or regret later?"**. Back to behaviors that help out in many aspects of my life from diet to exercise, the psychology of simply stating that it has to be one way or another really helps my stress showdown.

When we were trying to buy a home, we realized that saving was going to be a sacrifice at the time, but we didn't want to regret not having one later. Typically, no one wants to feel regret, so the choice is usually sacrifice. The awareness of the choice that must be made in order to fulfill a goal can certainly add some clean stress to your current situation, however it will also push you farther than you would have gone without it.

Another staple I use to combat dirty stress is to **never make decisions out of fear**. We have all heard the gotcha's stating certain situations where a deal will end if you don't act now, or an opportunity won't ever present itself again. There is no place for this type of dirty stress and the best way to clean it is just to avoid it.

Look at the decision again as dichotomous and tell yourself that if you are afraid of what could happen if you don't act, then the answer needs to be no. Just act as you have taken the stress showdown focus and changed it from lacking assertion to now having it. Once we regain control, then the stress is now clean and we can use that effort for productivity.

Times of great stress can also leave us in a state of mind called **survival mode** whereas we can really only focus on the two lower levels of needs (physiological and safety), which contributes to a limited scope of reality. Remember when animals are pushed into a corner (emotionally or physically) they fight to survive Being in survival mode is like wearing **growth blinders** and is detrimental to any type of long-term accomplishment. Keeping that in mind, I anticipate a direct correlation with how well your needs are being met and how far in the future you can plan or grow.

For lack of a better example, look at the homeless population. These people all have different situations and stories, however the thing they share is their inability to break out of survival mode. They are unable to experience growth and persevere due to the fact that their constantly worried about where their next meal is coming from and while sleeping on the streets or in shelters, they are constantly fearing for their safety.

It would be impossible for them to focus on getting a career started, let alone start a savings account. They are worried about the next 24 hours and that is all. Being in survival mode for the majority of us is not this extreme, but still it is holding us back in some capacity. If we are in a position where we feel trapped in a neighborhood that is going downhill or we are struggling to put food on the table, this equates to survival mode.

It is so important that if you are in a situation like this that you have enough awareness to affect some sort of change in your life. Complacency is the best friend of survival mode and again we revisit taking the power back and turning dirty stress to clean. It is vital that you do all you can to get to a better situation or you will wake up one morning 20 years down the road and wonder why this continues to be your reality. Use the clean stress of survival mode to better your situation to propel you to growth. On the flip side of this, professionals who retire with great benefits and monthly income, seemingly care deeply about climate change and the federal deficit.

I lived in survival mode for a considerable amount of time, specifically most of my time in Michigan. Once I had the awareness to create some change, I realized that in order to make a better life for my family I must increase my workload and limit my free time (back to sacrifice vs. regret). I heard an amazing story of a man out with his son in their truck looking for firewood. They were off-roading in late fall and the road conditions became worse with every second they continued to trek into the woods.

With my 10 years spent in Michigan I had frequent run-ins with cold weather, and being an Arizona native, I paid close attention to this story, making sure I was further prepared for the danger of winter. Not just acclimating to the cold, but also driving in snow and preparing for unforeseen situations. This involved making sure you had water bottles and blankets in the vehicle and also you needed to have functioning 4-wheel drive.

Back to the story at hand, the father and son had left the trail and found themselves stuck in mud as the ground hadn't completely frozen up yet. After a few tries of make shifting a way out, they decided to go ahead and begin collecting firewood. The man had called some friends to come help and figured they would make the most out of their incompetence and try something different. They decided to put branches of wood in the bed of the truck. As time went by, the bed of the truck became heavier and heavier and as I heard this story, I thought to myself that this is analogous to my relationship with stress.

Adding additional tasks or productive responsibilities to an already full slate, can manufacture clean stress that is helpful in development and the realization of goals. The wood that was put in the back of the truck served as a reminder that not only could the truck handle the additional load, the weight actually provided traction to the tires and there was no longer help needed to get the truck unstuck.

This story proved to be an extremely valuable lesson for me to understand that just because the responsibilities are mounting, the wood is still heavy and just because the truck makes it look easy, doesn't mean that it is. The additional load provides guidance! If we can take a situation like this and look at the positives, organize our perspectives and win the stress showdown, we are in prime condition to create positive change in our daily lives.

In one of my absolute favorite books, "The Happiness Advantage", by Shawn Achor, he states that if we are able to incorporate a positive view to stress our brains would be much better at problem solving and critical thinking, then if we were negative, neutral or stressed. A positive approach to stress shows us a path to greatness and allows for long lasting behavioral change or the ability to thrive. We will further discuss thriving and maximizing our individual potential in Chapter 5 of this book as I am using the preceding chapters to lay out a foundation of experiential awareness.

Spirituality:

I often wonder what my heavenly father has planned for me. When I was able to fully bring Christ into my life, I was spiritually lost and in desperate need for His help. My background in religion was borderline adversarial and I had no desire to make Church a part of my life. I felt like the addition of spirituality to complete Chapter 1 was a perfect chance to explain my journey and to also put an end to a chapter that focus' on more basic needs.

One of my first visits to Church, which was filled with speculation, provided the best message for my personal relationship with Christ and set me on my way to understand my Faith as an absolute necessity for growth. There was a story told by some members **I vividly remember, not what was said per se, but how it made me feel.**

It was a story told by Hugh Brown almost fifty years ago, began with a man who inherited a farm from a loved one, in an unfamiliar city and ended up relocating his family to start a new life there. The man pulled up to the house and noticed a large currant bush in the middle of the driveway and immediately thought that he needed to clean up the bush and he went to work. He pruned until nothing was left until sticks and stumps.

When the man finished with the work, he noticed that it looked like the tops of the stumps had beaded moisture as if the bush was crying. The story then proceeded to say, the man heard the bush saying to him that," it was disappointed that he decided to cut it down". "The currant bush explained that it was doing so well with growing and producing shade until the man came in and wrecked everything". "All the plants will now look down upon me". "How could you do this; you are supposed to be the gardener?"

The man proceeded to explain that, "he was the gardener here, and that he knows what he wants the bush to be. It was not to be a shade tree or to be liked by the other plants. It is to be a currant bush and one day when you produce fruit you will thank me by saying, thank you gardener for loving me enough to cut me down".

This analogy has resonated with me since hearing it as I have been through my fair share of disappointment and heartbreak. My wife and I had struggled to buy our first home, only for me to be laid off months after due to a down economy. We have struggled with potential health breakthroughs only to be riddled with disappointment after the relief was short term. We have all been through situations where we thought we were on the up and up, and just like that, the rug is pulled out from underneath us.

In times like these it is so incredibly important to understand God's plan for us. **Faith is not a typical deficient need; however, the lack of faith can hamper the development of the rest of the hierarchy.** We need to be comfortable with the idea that we don't know His plan, what trials we have in store or what mystery tomorrow will bring. We need to be grateful for blessings, as well as the trials that are put before us. Blessings are not a one size fits all that only benefit us in a real time manner. Trials need to be viewed as blessings as well, despite the ferocity and length of time it takes to view them as such.

When Blessings finally become clearer,
It's usually through the rearview mirror.

It is also extremely empowering to live in a place of gratitude, so that we can throw away the victim mentality. Knowing that our Heavenly Father has a plan for each of us is empowering and relieving. The tenth commandment states that we shouldn't covet what others have. What I have taken this to mean is that God doesn't love me less despite the fact that I see others having more than me. I take it as the fact that if I ask for blessings and don't receive them, all that means is that He is blessing the lives of others that I cannot see and that I need to understand the **blessings counterweight.** *Worry about yourself and your growth.*

The blessings counterweight means that I don't want to take away any goodness from others and I understand that there are plenty of blessings to go around. This type of humility for ourselves and love for each other is exactly what Christ had in mind for all of us.

Relinquishing control whilst remaining humble is such a valuable trait. The understanding that we have a creator and we are not the end all be all, is what keeps us humble. When times are at their most difficult, we need to look back and thank the gardener for loving us so much that he needed to cut us down and for caring about us so much that he needed to hurt us.

Each religion has their own moral codes in order to take care of the mind, body and spirit, while simultaneously honoring themselves and those around them. I am absolutely aware that is it possible to be guided by a moral compass while not conforming to the beliefs of any specific religion. The 10 commandments provide a clear path for Jews and Christians to follow Gods laws.

Christ made it much simpler and stated to love thy neighbor and to love thy God. If you look at yoga or the Hindu religion, therein lies a similar list of 10 principles that help to increase humility, develop inner peace and cultivate discipline. This list is called the Yama's and Niyama's and contains guidelines on: non-violence, truthfulness, non-stealing, non-possession, moderation, purity, austerity, purity, self-reflection and devotion to a higher being.

If you look at Buddhism, the Eight-Fold Path describes a way to reach Nirvana through rightness in: belief, resolve, speech, action, livelihood, effort, thought and meditation.

What proved so vital for me and my spiritual journey is that we were created and we are loved. Everyone has their own journey and everyone is going through their trials, but no matter how important we feel that our present situation is, it is only temporary. We are going through this life to experience and learn so that we can return to our heavenly father.

It is amazing to me to understand that all these religious trains of thought have so much in common, yet were developed with language obstacles, vast geographical barriers and in various times throughout history, yet all have a similar baseline of how we should treat ourselves and others.

In my view, knowing that this life is a school in a sense and we are constantly being tasked with learning, adjusting and growing, as loving, growing and learning is part of His plan, in order for us to return to Him. When we look at how children and adults learn, they take a slightly different approach. Children can learn from positive or negative reinforcement (rewards and punishment). Adults really only make changes from pain/heartbreak. **Heartbreak or hitting rock bottom, can allow for change as well as a thinning of the veil between how we see the world and gaining a better understanding of His plan for us**. Throughout the book, we will discuss the value of heartbreak and growth opportunities that are realized because of it.

We are here together to help one another get through this life. We are trying to be as Christlike as possible. That is why I added this section to Chapter 1, as it felt as though a spiritual connection is vital to our foundation of needs.

Having faith in a higher power helps us to get through the darkness and illuminates our path in times of weakness. Think back to situations in your life when you made it through somethings you thought were untenable. The belief that good things will come, is a way to view faith. **Sometimes faith is found following a broken heart, as being emotionally fractured allows us to look at things differently. Faith is the core of a persistent heart. Lean on it as often as possible!**

Summary:

- Beware Boiled Frogs
- Psychology of behavior change. Seek out multiple ways of incorporating behaviors from other aspects of your life, into your diet.
- Circle the wagons and create a diet path that works for you. Ex. Scheduling, frequency, urgency etc.
- Initially the brain rejects all change, as it is perceived as a threat.
- Exercise is psychologically valuable.
- Through the sweat comes connection
- Dopamine is a tool for long term behavioral change, creativity and problem solving.
- Use exercise as a way to meditate and see the value of simple tasking.
- Active-Introspection is a way to unlock the power of the subconscious. Let the subconscious do the heavy lifting!
- We are never more in tune with our bodies than when we are experiencing discomfort.

63

- Addiction is simply a way to allow outside factors to control our universe and manufacture consciousness.
- Consciousness is the real addiction!
- Cravings suffocate what is important.
- Awareness is key to prioritize what you really want and use that as ammunition to make long lasting change.
- Be aware of dirty consciousness and create clean consciousness.
- With any behavioral change a certain level of reinvention is necessary. It is important to not be surprised when this happens and to seek out support against relapse.
- Dirty stress is crippling and Clean stress is motivating.
- Look to your thoughts to control the physiological reaction caused by both types of stress.
- Stressful showdowns need to be looked at in a constructive manner in order to create clean stress.

- Survival mode is just like wearing growth blinders. Achieve a solid needs foundation, in order to reach potential.

- Adding more clean stress can be beneficial as it may add traction to our lives and help us stay on or find a better path.

- God loves us enough to hurt us and cut us down.

- Familiarize yourself with the blessings counterweight.

- Growth comes from heartbreak.

- Adults learn through heartbreak. Through pain comes growth.

- Thin your veil!

Chapter 2

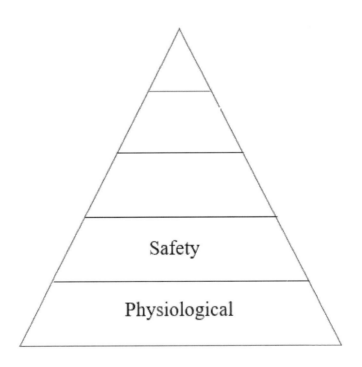

When looking at what we need in terms of safety, the following things come to mind: shelter, health, job security and a safe community. However, safety is so much more than those components. In the sections below, I wanted to go a bit deeper to really understand how our modern-day society sense of needs has changed as opposed to when this theory was written over 75 years ago.

- **Modulate the Flow of Information**
- **Safeguard your Worth**
- **Free Voice**
- **Financial Security**
- **Panning out the Gravel**

When we look at modulating the flow of information, it takes into consideration things that will benefit us contemporarily as well as long term. We need to differentiate the good from the bad when it comes to technology. The next section shows us the importance of qualifying relationships and identifying our worth and that of people we let in our circles. Then we proceed to talking about the importance of being able to speak your mind in all settings of your life, without possible judgements or ramifications. Financial security goes deeper than: spend less than you earn and depicts the struggles we go through in commercial America; and the decisions that go into when and where we consume our earnings. Lastly, we show the need to differentiate the things that don't matter in our external worlds, in order to isolate ourselves from things that could eventually prove meddlesome or harmful to what we deem safe.

Freedom Sanctuary

"Don't cry because it's over, smile because it happened!"
-Dr. Seuss

Modulate the Flow of Information:

My wife and I sat down with our children not so long ago and attempted to explain that despite technology being an extremely valuable tool, it is never to be used as a toy. We explained to them that we have a unique perspective on smart devices as we were born in a time where we had it both ways. Growing up in elementary and high school, my wife and I had to use maps to navigate, libraries to find research material and phone books to find the nearest specialty store or contact.

My children have no concept of this and it's no fault of their own. They have become entirely dependent on this gadget they hold in their hands to tell them how to do everything. They have become so reliant on this device that they feel as though everything that comes out of it is going to help them and must be accurate. This is the psychology of social media. The maps that the device produces lead me to where I want to go. The shopping apps I have allow me to buy things safely and they are delivered when they say they are supposed to. This should hold true with social media, right? Everything else should be safe and accurate, right?

I truly believe that when social media first was developed it was produced for all the right reasons. There

71

was no previously affordable way to connect with and keep in contact with family and friends from all over the country. In my experience it was such a help to know that I could still see what my friends were doing and to see photos of their kids without being in the same town. On the surface, it was a great tool.

Things have changed a bit now as people are growing an increased fondness to their devices and a reliance for positive affirmation from any social media platform. The advertisers are well aware of this fact. They begin to slowly show you things that you may be interested in and advertise to you; websites or products that you recently viewed. All of that data allows them to better understand what directs you to continue with the dopamine surplus, to keep you engaged. With social media constantly grooming you to trust all suggestions it makes; it is hard to take an objective approach to the data you are presented. With that being said, **it has never been more important in all aspects of your life to simply modulate or control the information that you consume.**

The information from social and all forms of media could certainly be spot on, but it is still vitally important to make sure you don't accept someone else's take without properly investigating and seeing both sides. It has never been more important to do your research and understand that there are many mediums to obtain information. It can be easy to follow whatever news station that confirms your view on specific topics. Or listen to a podcast from someone who you feel will agree with you, but that doesn't help the narrative. That is just you looking to feel validated and following others/groups who agree with you, in which you have a positive disposition towards; this is called the halo effect. **Don't take the path of least resistance, as we specifically and intentionally to seek out confirmation of our own narrative.**

When seeking out facts and truth, be an investigator. Watch a news station that leans a different way than you do politically. Read a book that is factually based and has sources to corroborate the statements. Just do your homework in order to better understand what is being thrown your way. **Don't be misled by how easy and trustworthy your device has become or take every bit of information as scripture. Be your own advocate**.

If you are using social media outside of the realm of fact-based inquiry and simply do not have a designated need for it, then what is the point of it? Every aspect of social media is a glorified way to use what real life has already mastered. You want to talk to someone, call, text, facetime or visit them. You just simply don't need all the other features that smart phones contain. Don't be afraid to seek out your own information. Delete those apps and notifications that someone else wants you to learn. It is someone else's agenda and you need to be award of this. Be your own objective curator.

One more thing to consider is that modulating the flow of information also means the speed at which we absorb content. Don't be afraid to receive new content at a traditional pace in order to reduce impulsivity and increase creativity. From a spiritual standpoint here, a quote comes to mind, **"if the devil can't make us sin, he will make us busy"**! Don't bother yourself with unproductive tasks and being in a hurry. Slow down and just be. **After all, not one place in the Bible does it mention that Jesus rushed. He was nothing but busy, and yet he walked everywhere!!**

There is an interesting story I heard at Church, whereas the early missionaries in the Congo were so excited to share Christianity with natives deep within the jungle. They hired guides that spoke the language and knew the terrain. About a week into the journey, the guides were falling behind and eventually stopped moving. When the missionaries found out what was going on, an interpreter stated that **they were moving too fast and their souls couldn't keep up**! I took this as extremely profound as I feel as though I am way too busy for my soul to keep up! Try to have a **Slow Soul!**

Every semester I ask my undergraduate students to write down an extravagant goal that they have held onto for quite a while, but haven't yet acted upon (there is no reason why you at home couldn't do the same). Ultimately, some goal that they have put a pin in. I ask all the students to write it down and share with the peers around them. This ask of vulnerability can seem a bit daunting to some, but eventually they get over it.

At that point, I ask them to write down a path that they could achieve this goal by identifying what is missing out of their lives that they need in order to make it happen. I give examples of what kind of support is needed and what kind of roadblocks they anticipate experiencing. Without fail, almost every single student in every class comes back to the same thing being needed, more time!

Once they all relay the information to me about being able to achieve this crazy goal if they only had more time, I proceed to ask them to pull out their phones and look at the screen time setting and to tell me what they see. Usually at this time, some students break into laughter or just begin to shrink in their seat. I tell them that each and every one of us gets the same amount of time in a day and we have to choose how to best spend that time.

With many of the students, they seem to be embarrassed by the fact that they saw numbers from 2, 4, 6 even 8 hours a day worth of screen time. I know we discussed awareness in the previous chapter, and it is going to be alive and well throughout this book. In order to make and affect positive change in your life, you have to be aware of prior shortfalls in order to know where to go.

Also, don't be afraid to read physical books and handwrite notes. This age-old activity has many seemingly forgotten benefits. When you read you process the information at YOUR pace, no distractions, no power struggles. It's YOUR pace! When you hand write things, if forces you to slow down and accurately represent your thoughts and feelings. My handwriting is absolutely awful, so when I force myself to write things, I clear my mind and produce content. When you hold books or a pen/paper, you are also initializing different learning modalities. Feeling the weight of the book, holding the writing instrument, touching the texture of pages can be quite the opportunity for creativity, if you let it in.

When you regulate what comes your way, you are providing a psychologically safe environment to learn

and grow. You are not constantly looking over your shoulder at the emotional fallout of being fed the wrong information. If you can change the lens in which you view your outside world then you can be aware of the changes you must make in order to be at minimum, adequately receptive and in the know.

Safeguard your Worth:

The next section speaks to the value of healthy relationships, not in regard to connection and compassion as we will take more time with that in chapter 3, but the destruction of abusive relationships and how to persevere and overcome. We all have experienced unfavorable relationships either firsthand or at a distance, and hopefully this section of the chapter will help to see a way to be safe and grow in our relationships.

All relationships come down to a relationship with ourselves. How do you react to certain situations and what is the outcome? What I learned is that I needed to understand my own worthiness and create boundaries and distance, to eventually stop the cycle. With the creation of boundaries, it has taught me that you cannot change people. People are people, for better or worse. You can change however, how you think and feel about yourself and your relationship. As I mentioned earlier, all relationships are a relationship with yourself. You choose your level of interaction and engagement.

For most, it is easier to play the victim than to seek out a positive resolution. If we look back to Chapter 1 and think about how we can apply the clean stress to this situation, the first thing that comes to mind is to reconcile our choices. Let's not forget that having a victim mentality is giving others the power over our choices, which makes us feel like a victim and powerless. If we apply clean stress to our relationships, we can have control over our own emotions and feel empowered.

We all are part of relationships, some may be healthier than others, however we are still in them. What is the difference between relationships where we are able to flourish vs. relationships where we are anxious and insecure? I feel that the difference in our relationships lies within the **expectations we set** and **getting in front of issues** and not letting them dictate. I used to have a coworker who would consistently come into the office 10 minutes late. Literally like clockwork. Me on the other hand, was typically 10 minutes early. Then one day I was a few minutes late and it was like the sky was falling. I was asked to talk to my boss privately and concern was shared. In this instance, expectations were not met and my coworkers had a hard time with it. With the alignment of expectations come the ability to be more vulnerable in the future.

Anticipation of how others will respond to situations comes from a lifetime of lived events that prepare us for what comes next. Start looking for evidence of actions that live in situations and expect them. This will limit the confusion and the number of surprises. Conversely, if you communicate your expectations to others, then it will entice them to live up to what you expect from them.

We all have an **owner's manual** and we all know what makes us tick and how we ourselves operate within specific scenarios. However, this manual should be viewed as situational and expectations need to be communicated and/or agreed upon as to what will be shared vs not shared. Owner's manuals are not transferable, just think of different car variations. Your manual works for your car. It is not universal and must be communicated with others (as well as having others share with us) in order to have quality interactions. This manual will include our definition of kindness, respect, loyalty, inappropriateness etc. With that being said, also keep in mind that **it is not your responsibility to correct someone's misunderstanding of your owner's manual, just make sure to maintain transparency!**

If we look at the scenario of taking your shoes off in someone's home, how do you view that? I have lived in Arizona as well as Michigan and I can tell you that wearing shoes in your home in Arizona is not a big deal, but wearing them in Michigan is definitely an issue. There are cultural and geographic expectations that we form in order to contribute to our manual that no one is going to know, unless it is discussed.

Another example that comes to mind is being on time. I am a punctual person and the importance of being somewhere according to the plan was engrained in my being at an early age. I view people being late as rude, insensitive and that there is not a value placed on my time. The flip side of this, is that I know a lot of people who are constantly late and they think nothing of it. There are even people who tell guests that an event will be starting thirty minutes earlier than it is, in knowing that the invitees will not be on time.

Again, it is all about communication and we need to be able to identify or get in front of the relationships that are truly important to us. There are key attributes that we must be on the lookout to identify quality relationships. Things like trust, loyalty, shared view on family, communication and honesty are paramount for a long-lasting relationship.

In most instances, we only allow ourselves to receive the amount of love that we feel we deserve. We need to be aware of this and put ourselves in a better situation in order to understand our own worth. However, in regard to allowing a safe space to develop and to continue to climb the needs pyramid, we are all worthy, because we are human!

When I think of worth, I picture a $100 bill and apply it to everyone. Some of us may be an old crumply $100 bill that is weathered and hasn't looked fresh and new in years. Other $100 bills may be soggy from being left in the washer, inside of a pair of jeans or have a slight tear from being pulled out of a billfold too fast.

No matter how you view the $100 bill, you are still worth $100. That value is never taken away. You are certainly worthy of love and affection. You are worthy of happiness! Keep this in mind as you make sure that your relationships are worthy of you.

Partnerships also have weight when it comes to being worthy. When in a relationship, others must also view you as being worth $100. An interesting way to view this is that if you value yourself at $100 and you view your partners worth at $100 there is an even exchange and expectations are typically met.

If your partner views you at less than $100 and you view them at $100, you may begin to feel insecure and anxious about the longevity of the relationship. If you view your worth at $100 and you view your partners at less than $100, you may not feel as though your time and attention are warranted. There must a level of equivalence when it comes to successful relationships.

As a metaphor, I often think of the Panama Canal, and how it coincides with worth. As a quick aside, the canal is comprised of locks in which water must be added to one lock as it is taken away from another, in order to allow passage of ships through the canal. This takes place multiple times, as the water levels must be equal in order for the process to work. Just like with relationships and worth, the water level must be in harmony in order to reach the desired result.

Shy away from doubting your Worth,
Simply because you were put here on Earth

Free Voice:

This section looks to convey the need that we must feel safe to communicate our opinions and beliefs, without the fear of recourse. Our voice is not just the sounds and air leaving our mouths, but our perspectives and insight as well. In some instances, I even have a hard time with revision or editing my writing, as I feel that my initial voice is the one that I want heard and any changes could take away my voice.

Once we feel as though our opinion matters, we can begin to develop thoughts and actions that go far beyond what we previously thought was possible. In the book by Amy Edmondson, "The Fearless Organization", it depicts situations in our personal and professional lives that allow us to speak up without the being afraid of or humiliated by the perception of others.

This again boils down to the fact that we as individuals are worthy. We don't find our worth from the feedback of others. We don't find our worth from gaining or losing respect from our peers. We are already worthy. Why "Psychological Safety" is so valuable, is it provides a runway to develop our self-esteem that will eventually allow for growth. There is no need for negative consequences when we are trying to problem solve or critically think. In these situations, we must be able to generate our best ideas free of the dirty stress created by perceived social risk taking.

Try and remember situations in your life when you have been free of negative feedback which allowed for a productive and ultimately fun discussion on how to cure, fix or solve something. Now I want you to visualize all the people who were around you at the time. Identifying those exact people or similar individuals, as who you need to surround yourself in order to feel worth from being respected and accepted. I suggest you do this exercise often to try and relive the experiences that bring the best out of you and others, in order to focus on who was there to bring out your best. Then replicate as often as possible. If we understand the set (people and mindset) and setting (environment and situation) of when we were successfully vulnerable, that experience will transfer to give confidence to be vulnerable in less familiar scenarios.

With every situation that is beneficial or constructive, we need to discuss the likelihood of potentially harmful situations. It seems to me that the individuals who hate on creativity or try to shine a light on potential inadequacies are ones who never put themselves out there. It makes no sense to me that people who have nothing better to do, but to troll around and pick apart your visions, have no intention of ever doing anything that warrants vulnerability.

Contemporary literature has done a great job in the last few years with bringing awareness to the value of being vulnerable. One of my favorite authors, Brené Brown has done some amazing research on the fact that becoming more vulnerable leads to more risk taking and higher rewards. In her book, "Daring Greatly", she further states that you cannot achieve great things without taking great risks. This reminds me of the quote, "Don't be afraid to go out on a limb, its where all the fruit is!".

Taking risks aren't just reserved for a young man,
Perhaps just having balls, is a good enough plan!

We will further discuss the value of vulnerability in the next chapter as we go deeper into the value of relationship and human connection. The main thing I want you to take away from this segment is that you have to **put yourself out there** if you want to apply for a promotion that you are underqualified for (in my opinion if you are qualified for a job, that means you are overqualified). You have to put yourself out there if you want to talk to a stranger at a party or tell someone you have strong feelings for them. Having a safe environment to take chances is what it is all about, and the more you do it, the easier it becomes.

I tell my wife a joke about how in order to finally feel comfortable with growing a mustache, it takes twelve separate instances of growing one. It is not my fault that a certain industry ruined mustaches for eternity, however I am quite fond of them. Where I am going with this is, that all new behaviors take some getting used to. Nothing that matters is going to be easy, but you still need to try! Half of the battle is knowing that it will be an uphill climb. I find that when my expectations don't align with the outcome, I typically have a hard time dealing with the results. Knowing that failure is inevitable in a safe environment will allow you the ability and courage to be resilient and persevere.

The key to this is that **before you become vulnerable and truly put yourself out there, you need to be comfortable with both possible outcomes.** I recently applied for a position (which I did not get) and was getting ready for my 6th interview, and my wife and I joked, "holy crap, what if I get it!" Would I have been ready for that outcome? Hopefully yes, however it's moot.

If you are considering telling someone how you feel about them, you need to make sure that you get in front of all potential scenarios so that you are safe within the outcome. If you are wanting to have a difficult discussion with someone who means a lot to you, go over the scenarios in your head so that no matter the outcome you have prepared for it and you can put yourself out there again. This is an added benefit of closure as it makes sense, you allowed yourself to practice multiple feelings about the situation and you are able to accept multiple results.

The last thing you want when being vulnerable is to not fully understand the gravity of a situation and deal with adversity so severe that it impacts your ability to be vulnerable in the future. **If you are not ok with specific outcomes, do not try, but go back to a scenario that is safer and build your confidence. Revisit the trying situation at a later date when more prepared**. We will go over more thought work in Chapter 5, but the scenarios provided allow for an overview of why being safe and vulnerable is important.

When thinking about what the naysayers will write or how others will view your work, you need to remember what Theodore Roosevelt said about putting yourself out there. He said that, "It is not the critic who counts or the man who points out how the strong man stumbles". Those people don't matter because they are not doing anything bold or brave! The only people who matter are the ones that understand what you are going through because they have also gone through it. Keep all of this in mind as trolls and eBallers pop up during vulnerable times, to try and disrupt your flow and vision and steal your psychological safety!

How trolls and eBallers affect us is they state their own opinions and judgements, then we proceed to look for evidence of truth. If someone said, your blue hair is hideous, this might not affect you at all since you don't have blue hair. If someone were to say that they don't like our eye color, we may find evidence that we don't like our eye color. With the evidence of truth lies the internal suggestion of our flaws and weaknesses. We think to ourselves, "if they can see it, then others can too". You begin to look for evidence that your eyes are ugly or that they look strange. Hence you may begin to believe that you don't like your eyes. People believe that what others think, is who they are.

Being confident in safe situations provide suitable practice for the ability to bounce back from true adversity. **We are simply going to be as vulnerable as we feel safe**. Once we master the ability to put ourselves out there with tougher crowds in tougher environments, then and only then are we able to show our truly authentic selves!

Holding in feelings and emotions in order to help or protect others is not the answer for sustainable relationships.

Something most typically gives. It is tough to think of situations where an individual loves someone so much that they would rather bear all the pain and anguish, in order to protect the other person from pain, reputational impact, scrutiny etc.

Decide What to Be and Go Be It,

Head full of doubt/Road full of Promise,

-Avett Brothers

I had a friend that was suffering from intense alcohol addiction and his main concern was telling his girlfriend that he had an issue. His fear of transparency overtook the fear of the addiction he suffered from. He ended up coming clean and his now fiancé was incredibly supportive and they are now thriving as a couple. Key takeaways from this is to not suppress your feelings in order to help others. Utilize your free voice as transparency is crucial with partnership equivalence, leading to psychological safety.

"Everything you've ever wanted, is sitting on the other side of fear."

-George Addair

Ultimatums can also be used in these types of situations; however, you must understand the ramifications and be 100% prepared to carry out the message. It is almost like how you would treat a child and understand that if your bluff is called and you are not prepared to follow through, you have just used your one and only shot at tactical advantage. This can also be difficult as when ultimatums are discussed amongst partnerships in order to specifically change behaviors alone; this will lead to relationship failure. The goal must be to change the thoughts and feelings leading up to the behavioral change and typically most times thoughts accompany pain/heartbreak.

When we look at trying to create/maintain control over situations, I think back to a great read, titled "I Used to be a Miserable F*ck", by John Kim, The Angry Therapist. He posits that without compassion there can be no control. He further states, that **when you practice compassion, you not only share your unconditional love to help another, but you are then more open to receiving love back. You then grow in soul and spirit and turn from a cold stone into a reflective prism.**

Situations can be difficult; however, you never want to take away someone else's pain as it is not just the pain you are shouldering. As we discussed in previous chapters, from pain and heartbreak come growth and development. **You may think that you are helping someone by taking their pain from them, but in actuality, you are taking away their opportunity to grow.** It takes courage to allow someone to go through stages of grief or emotional processing. The opportunity for growth may be for the one allowing the pain as well as the one going through it. Growth is not one-sided.

The stages are: denial, anger, bargaining, depression and lastly acceptance. Some of my prior students have labeled me as being sadistic, when in actuality I don't want anyone to suffer, as I know that a direct result of pain is betterment. However, this next sentence is for comic relief, but I will also joke as I look forward to individuals to be depressed whilst processing their emotions and/or grief. I understand the sequence and that means that they are close to acceptance and almost done with the stages! :)

Financial Security:

Our society feeds on the fact that we can send information real time to anywhere in the world. This could be an advertisement for an exciting new phone or a picture of someone standing beside their new car. Because we have access to all of this information at our fingertips, it could potentially lead to impulsivity and jealousy. The invention of credit certainly has its positives like being able to pay for a home or a car over time, but the issue is that it also affords us the ability to stretch ourselves too thin.

One of my favorite sayings is, **"You can never have too much of the things you don't need".** With the assumption that our basic needs are met, we then delve into luxury land and further extend ourselves financially. The cycle is created that if I just work a little harder, then I will make more money and I can pay more for something. The issue is that this behavior doesn't stop and we constantly want more and more. There is a relevant TedTalk from the Minimalists, they state the importance of really acquiring what you need and finding ways to appreciate what you have and to find a career that supports that mode of spending. This type of awareness is paramount in realizing our basic needs and having a fulfilled life.

I have fell prey to this and I am sure many of you have as well. However, enough is enough. When my wife and I got married, we didn't have the proverbial, pot or a window. We were in love and we were going to make a go of it. We would dream about someday owning a home or having a new/reliable car (forget luxury). I remember thinking that if I could only have a job where I could make the amount of money that I make today, that we would be completely set and not need a cent more.

Slowly but surely, we would achieve a little bit more and would move into a better neighborhood and had nicer things. Only to find ourselves longing and wanting what others have. This bit us in the rear, every time we found ourselves climbing the social ladder. It continues to baffle me that as the years go by and the success mounts, for some reason the goals change. We continue this level of progression and we continually put the carrot just a bit further out in front.

It is a tough concept to appreciate what others have while not wanting it for yourself. It is certainly not a big deal to be happy for someone who has nicer things as long as you wish for it for yourself. Where we get into trouble here is when we don't think they deserve it or when jealousy comes into play. We need to be able to view success as two vases filled to the same height with sand and when one person gets more sand it doesn't mean that they take sand from us. We need to view it as more sand has been added. Stay away from keeping up with the Jones', as the cycle will never end.

As I mentioned in the previous section, I recently had applied for a leadership promotion, and it would be more money and more clout, however there would be considerably more time and effort required to excel. Still, I pushed myself to apply and hone in my skills and accomplishments in order for the real me to reflect my resume.

After I found out that I didn't get the position, I went through the stages of grief (like clockwork), then when I finally got to stage five and accepted the outcome, I had a realization. I remembered back to when I was a new husband and father and recalled how amazing it would be just to be in the spot that I am in now.

Not only did I immediately feel gratitude for my success, I decided to begin to work hard again to get to where I am now. I call this **Static Ambition**. It isn't just the thrill of finding new things or achievements, it is also striving for things that you currently have and hope to maintain. Try to change your view and really work hard and strive for the things you currently have. Long for the job, house and family you have now. Typically, we strive for newness, can you look back and identify the last time you applied a focused active pursuit towards having the things you already have? Ambition is typically only relevant in regards to happiness, joy and/or fulfillment until we have our needs met. At that point, your happiness stops leveling up and begins to level off.

There is nothing wrong with the active pursuit of what you already have. It is all about changing the perspective and the finish line. You can make success look however you want, so why not turn back the clock to a prior you and view your current situation through those eyes?

A clear and real issue that faces many professionals is the issue of burnout and honestly, it is more of a state of simultaneous boredom and unfulfillment. When dirty stress is alive and well in our lives and we have limited to no handle on the outcome, there is a good chance we are experiencing early stages of burnout. When we transition from dirty stress to clean stress (viewing it as a challenge), we limit the effects of burnout and have a much more productive view of our contributions. **Stress is not the only component of burnout, as we must also consider a negative sense of self, negative response to our job and cynicism.**

The awareness of dirty stress coupled with the ability to view it through a new lens allows us to take a new perspective and approach to the tedious and mundane. In

Chapter 5 of this book we will go into more detail about how our thoughts affect the results of our lives, as this chapter is designed to provide a realization of what is possible if we truly appreciate what we have.

Another great topic I feel that it is important to discuss in regard to finances, is the concept of **revering house money**. As a quick recap, house money is when you have successfully gambled your own money and have used winnings to continue on, instead of your own money, viewing it as a bonus, as you are no longer risking personal capital. House money can be an added benefit to maximize your current situation or you can tuck it away for later use. In this section, be thinking of ways to do both in a coinciding manner.

This concept takes into consideration that you are going to treat your life now as you know it will end at some point, but also to leave a little in the tank for later. I know from personal experience we look at our lives as either trying to live in the moment and try to be present, or we find ourselves preparing and saving for the future or what we will be able to do once we stop working.

One of my good tennis buddies had stomach cancer when he was forty. The only reason he was alerted to it, is because he was adopted and had no idea of his family medical history and was insistent that he would do physicals every few years. Turns out, he was right in being proactive and he was able to early detect a cancer that would have taken his life. At this point he now views every day as playing with house money.

Another brief story was when I first got married, my wife was very ill, and we found ourselves just trying to get by one day at a time. There was no desire to put money in a 401(k) or to even have a savings account, as we were knee deep in survival mode. We didn't know where the next year would lead us so we did the best we could to appreciate our relationship in real time. Now, after 15 years of marriage, we have transitioned to being able to more or less do both. **Sometimes it appears as though thriving is merely surviving.**

Studies have shown that happiness levels appear in a U-shaped curve and that we are happiest in the beginning and end of our lives. That is a perfect example of how to revere house money; find the balance between being prepared and being present. Don't be afraid to add additional perspective to this process. Speak to older people who are in the winter of their lives. They just might surprise you with their insight and attitudes towards many of the daunting questions that are currently troubling you.

Personally, we have savings and retirement, but at the same time we spend money like we may not be around in 20 years. I believe this perspective is important and a healthy financial balance is paramount. Make a concerted effort to spend time with your loved ones and let work take a back seat. Revering house money can allow you to look at your life now as you would at the end. **Work and/or your career is a renewable resource. Time and Love are not.**

Measure your fortune in adventure and time,
That's a schilling that needs no polish to shine!

Take a quick second to think about the grass in your front yard, or at a nearby park. Now think about grass and how many things it can do without outside influence. There are literally two things it is capable of, it can grow or it can die. It doesn't remain static or status quo. View your approach to joy and fulfillment in this manner. It does not remain constant, it will either grow or die. Constantly work to develop your financial security, as well as balance in all things, as psychological strengths need continuous cultivation.

Don't forget that the most addictive things in this world are heroin and a paycheck!

99

Panning out the Gravel:

There are distractions all around us that limit us from focusing on what we want/need. In a physiological sense, distractions can be good, as cavemen needed to be aware of the tiger in the bushes as he approached a stream or the awareness of any type of imminent danger. As we have evolved in the twenty-first century, distractions limit our potential and allow others to dictate our actions and fate.

Keep in mind that when our brains process emotion, there is no tense (past, present or future) involved. It is only seen as a real time threat. The dirty pain of stress and anxiety from last week, when relived, cause the same type of harm as they did when they happened. Memories and the anticipation of negative emotions are processed as real time threats as the epinephrine and cortisol are filling up your blood stream.

This takes me back to my view of social media and how we need to be very cautious/rid ourselves of it. If we take Facebook and scroll through a normal page, what do we see? I deactivated my account because there were there were so many things that brought out emotions I didn't want to experience at that given time. I would be scrolling and see a child that was terminally ill and asking for a donation to help out with medical bills. My immediate reaction is sadness and then I was shaming myself as I couldn't help out financially or in any other charitable manner. I certainly wanted too, but I was just not in a position to help. These real time emotions didn't have a place in my normal day and I had to find a way to remove them from my life. It is not that I don't care or want to help. I do plenty around my community financially and by volunteering my time, I am just not in a position to help everyone in need that I see on Facebook.

I realized that situations like this, that brought about these negative emotions had no place in my life and were suffocating the emotions that I wanted to feel, hijacking the direction of my day. I have found myself feeling empathy burnout and limiting resources that I need to utilize for my more immediate milieu! This is where I made the switch in my life that I was only going to participate in activities that were a value add. In other words, I was only going to partake in experiences that were going to contribute to my growth or make me a better person.

Another great book by Shawn Achor, "Before Happiness", he discusses how noise can get in the way of our growth. All of the time wasted, and negative feelings felt on social media or less productive activities are all just noise in my life and I now strive to limit the noise and to become more aware of when it is present.

I now look at it like I am **panning out the gravel** or panning for value (gold) and the gold is all value-added activities that I now strive for. I am now aware of what to look for and the model I use is to drain all the noise or gravel out of the pan and all that is left, is the gold or value that I am looking for. The more we practice this and fine tune our lens, the easier it is moving forward.

Another type of noise is when people are full of hot air and depict flakey behaviors. There is no value add to people telling you what you want to hear and then taking it back at a later date. I am sure we all know or have known someone who is a people pleaser and will tell you what you want to hear or make plans with you, only to cancel or change their minds at the last minute. Be aware of people pleasers as they are ultimately liars. I believe they have positive intentions in the beginning, only to take an easy way out, down the road.

People pleasers are the relationship version of noise, and they will continue to cause you harm unless the appropriate actions are taken. It is important in all relationships, that healthy boundaries are created so that the expectations of both parties are realized. With upfront discussions that could potentially be uncomfortable, it will produce healthy relationships, despite the length of being involved. If we suffer from the anxiety of instigating these tough conversations, just consider that **whenever you are not able to address your authentic self you are delaying the unavoidable, and all you are losing is time.** This theory is transferable to other parts of your life, like changing jobs or making tough choices. **Don't sacrifice your time on delaying a tough conversation that you are going to inevitably have (unrenewable resource)!** We can go back to being dichotomous; would you rather stall and delay or would you rather salvage the time you are at risk of losing?

One strategy I use in order to ensure that I am finding enough value in my activities is to be aware of the 1x1 rule. This rule states that for every hour I do something less productive, I spend the same amount of time being productive. If I spend an hour consuming content on my phone, I must spend an hour producing an experience or activity. If I spend an hour texting, I must spend the same amount of time handwriting notes, letters, etc. (remember we already discussed the value in holding a pen/paper and writing). One hour watching fiction = one hour of watching non-fiction, documentaries or biographies. Lastly, if I spend an hour watching sports, I must spend an hour doing sports or exercising.

In an extremely insightful book by Sarah Knight, "The Life-Changing Magic of Not Giving a F*ck", she mentions that we need to seek out value in the form of our "f*cks" and each of us have a **"f*ck budget", as in this sense "f*cks" are being allocated as time, energy and money.** If we can identify the true intention of our "f*cks", then we will certainly have panned out the gravel. So, I ask you here and now to truly take a look at where you are dispersing your "f*ck budget", and ask yourself if it is being used in a manner you are happy with, is there another way you would like to use these resources and lastly, how can you better approach a plan to dispense these extremely valuable resources?

In order to bring this full circle with my students, an activity I like to do with my students is to watch a quick video on a recent children's movie, highly ingratiated with psychology. The movie depicts an accurate representation of emotional development. We first discuss the difference between beliefs and values. **Beliefs are more experiential and contextual, whereas values are intertwined with what is important to us from a needs base at any given time in our lives (typically fluid).** I look to integrate values with identify to have the students identify 5 key components of value/identity that they foresee being unshakeable. Some can even view this as a sacred value, whereas you are willing to fight or even die for them.

This is a great exercise to uncover value in your lives keep them front and center and/or top of mind.

Summary:

- Be aware of your environment and modulate the information you consume.
- Technology is a tool, not a toy.
- Seek out differing perspectives in order to fully align your objectivity.
- Be your own curator
- This applies to content and speed.
- Have a Slow Soul!
- Remove the convenience feature (notifications, apps) from your devices.
- Actively pursue at a normal pace.
- All relationships we have, are a relationship with ourselves.
- Understand that you cannot change people, but you can change how you view the relationship.
- Share your owner's manual.
- Seek out partnership equivalence and a better understanding of expectations.
- We are all worthy of love and affection.

- Witness set and setting that allowed for high levels of creativity and problem solving, in order to replicate.
- Seek out transparency and authenticity in relationships.
- Don't steal opportunities for others to grow, despite looking to help.
- Surround yourself with individuals that have been an integral part of previous success.
- Vulnerability breeds high risk, with even higher rewards.
- I'm only going to be as vulnerable as I feel safe to be.
- Sometimes thriving is merely the ability to survive.
- You can never have too much of the things you don't need.
- Beware of the carrot and be aware of the minimalist philosophy.
- Static Ambition-pursuit of what already exists.
- Fulfillment/joy transfer to top of bell curve.

- Revere house money, balance and end game vs now game.
- Understanding importance of professional contribution and how it relates to burnout.
- Focus the majority of your time and effort on resources that are not renewable.
- Limit distractions
- Our brains only process emotions in the present tense.
- Understand empathy burnout.
- Seek value, not gravel in your life. Understand what will help you vs. what will hurt you.
- 1x1 rule of uncovering the value.
- Don't sacrifice your time on delaying a tough conversation that you are going to inevitably have!
- How are you planning on spending your "f*ck budget" (time, energy and money)?
- Beliefs vs Values/Identity, keep them top of mind to easily find value.

Chapter 3

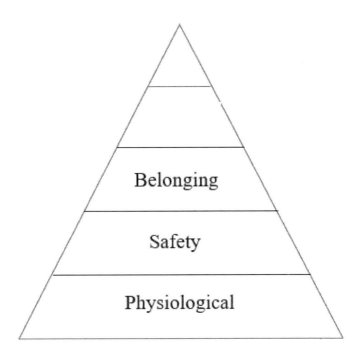

The third tier of the need's hierarchy talks about how once physiological and safety needs are met; we can look to strengthen our bonds with others around us. These bonds can include things like: strengthening friendships, finding intimacy and starting a family. But what else goes into our need to belong and love/be loved? What was missed in this initial assessment?

- **Foundational Relationships**
- **Value Added Attachments**
- **Reflect Recognition**
- **Extreme Feats of Kindness**
- **Perpetuation of Real-Life Interactions**

In the segments above, I have described some situations that I have went through and how I classified them in terms of value and warrant. As we move through this chapter we will discuss how to identify and stabilize value in our relationships, while discussing the history and importance of parental impacts. We will discuss different types of relationships and the value that each category brings and show the authenticity that love can unveil. We will then look into why we help others and creating a way to desire to do it more, to create a long-lasting trigger for charitable giving.

Lastly in this chapter, we will look at creating more in person interaction and the benefit it holds. Showing how technology and disconnection can paradoxically lead us astray.

Human Exchange

"Truth is everyone is going to hurt you: you just gotta find the ones worth suffering for"
-Bob Marley

Foundational Relationships:

Now that we have made it to the third level of this book, we can assume that we have a plan to maintain and progress past our physiological and safety needs. This section of the need's assessment discusses the value to relationships which Maslow viewed as a deficient need in his book, "A Theory of Human Motivation". What is pretty remarkable is that he was able to identify this theory back in 1943, when I believe most of society was experiencing issues with meeting their own psychological and safety needs.

In a time when we are more simultaneously connected and disconnected than ever, the importance for social support has never been greater. We begin in this world, with one or hopefully two parents and that is our first experience with understanding the value of love and belonging. The way they treat us, the way they allow others to treat them (and us) and the way they talk to themselves (and us), teaches us our early beliefs about ourselves.

If those beliefs don't foster acceptance and love of ourselves or those around us, then we may have unintentionally cultivated challenging relationships with ourselves and others in the future. Love and acceptance need to happen from within. If it doesn't happen as a child from the keystone relationships of parents and immediate family, then we need to go through some coaching or therapy in order to find the awareness of what is limiting ourselves, in order to find it from within. **We must have a feeling of love and belonging in order to set us up for success and growth throughout our lives.**

If these skills were not realized at an early age, I suggest making a cataLYST or a list from a person who precipitates an event (not as clever when you have to explain it), of all what was lacking in our youth and who was responsible for not giving us what we needed. This LYST can include things that we have held onto for quite some time that sporadically requires our attention.

This LYST can be formulated with the intention of forgiving those who caused us pain or deprived us of some developmental need. Despite now knowing that growth comes from pain and that we don't want to remove the opportunities for growth of ourselves and others, it is still a good idea to create this physical LYST in order to first forgive individuals from our past. Forgiveness is literally a financial term that means to relieve debts. The growth that can come from this type of action is excellent for forgiving others, but this can also be transferable and have efficacy with forgiveness of ourselves. We talked in Chapter 2 about all relationships starting with ourselves, this is another way to clear the air and move forward clean. Forgiveness and trust are not the same thing. In order to heal, it may be beneficial to compartmentalize trust and forgiveness of those who had foundational roles in our lives, in order to heal and progress with one thing at a time.

It is during the early years that we develop negative or positive self-talk, depending on how we were spoken to. If you don't have love and belonging around you or within you, then it is going to be much more difficult to put yourself out there and experience vulnerability. This is why having a solid foundation of love and belonging needs to happen first, before you are able to develop appropriate levels of self-esteem, which we will discuss in the next chapter. **Ultimately, vulnerability is not one foot in and one foot back. It is not having a safety net and is not having a just in case!**

Each one of us is worthy, however if we are not taught or eventually learn that, we will not develop self-esteem. This doesn't stop with our immediate family, as it is necessary to belong and be an active part of a community. It can come from peer groups, church memberships and forming romantic attachments in order to sustain the desire to belong and feel close to others.

I think back to when things drastically changed in our country, when inflation was out of control in the 70's (we are currently at a 31-year inflation high as well, according to the Wall Street Journal, Nov 21) and the country began to desperately need two incomes in the home. The lack of increased wages coupled with the need to have more of and better things, led families to seek out ways to improve their economic standing. More and more women went back to work and we began to see more and more unsupervised children.

There was also the women's liberation movement in the 70's which sought out equal rights, wages, opportunities and personal freedom for women. Sascha Cohen of Time magazine in 2015, published a great piece stating the benefits of this movement. In addition to workplace sex equality, title IX passed in 1972, and forbade sex discrimination in women's collegiate athletics. All things considered, it was time of great change and personal/familial/professional ambition.

I am in no way judging, my parents both worked and my dad was in the Army and traveled half the year. I am just making a point that this is when things began to shift. Around the same time, was when we started to see another revolution pop up, the video game revolution. This was a time when people of all ages were beginning to start heavily interacting with technology and virtual connections were born at an astounding rate.

The lack of supervision in the home had led to a lack of guidance of many children growing up in the '80's. This is alarming to me as we have seen the desensitization from our youth brought on by video games in the past, that have presumably led to horrific actions. My further worry is that we are now seeing another revolution with the relationships with our devices superseding the value of face-to-face connection.

We went from mothers being home for emotional support of the children after school and events. The father was typically around in the evenings, but the mother was so extremely important to the emotional development of the children. With mothers leaving to return the workplace, the children were desperately searching for connection and guidance and were going to find it somewhere, whether it was a video game or with friends. **The development of the youth was no longer provided by the figures that mattered most, and in my opinion, this was a dark spot for our culture.**

We put materialistic value ahead of the development of our most valued asset, our children. I don't think we

119

realized the impact this would have, and I feel that looking back we now know more than ever; we recognize how important the development of our youth is. These children are now parents and have come full circle to take a better approach to raising their children.

In the current landscape (Covid-19 Pandemic), where parents are able to be home more as companies are allowing different working options, as multiple video platforms have sprung up, allowing for an in person feel to the workplace. These options are allowing heightened quantity of time at home for all members of the family. We just need to make sure that even though we are physically home, we must ensure that we are mentally, spiritually and emotionally present as well. We are also currently knee deep in what is deemed, **"The Fatherless Generation", whereas despite dad's being home they may not really be home**. Dad's across the globe certainly need to step up their game!

I do not believe that women belong at home in the kitchen. That is not what I am saying. However, mothers are extremely valuable to society by being emotionally available to their children. My wife has worked full time most of our marriage. We are now in a time where kids need their parents more than ever, as cyberbullying and social media trolling has never been more prevalent. It is so important for children to have a solid foundation of family to lean on and seek advice. I do see things changing now as more and more parents are both working from home and we are certainly leaning toward correcting the issues of past generations. Technology certainly does have its advantages as working remotely allows us to get our children off to school as well as pick them up. We are able to provide real time help and solution development for our children, to help them know core moral baselines. **It all starts in the home and family has never been more important.**

When I mentioned that this aspect of human motivation is a deficient need, I was speaking specifically about the fact that we typically see issues arise with love and belonging when the aspects for the individual are deprived. When not deprived or even fulfilled, that is when the individual has achieved what is needed to move up to the next level and closer to growth. Also, **when you have your own needs met, that is when you are able to focus on helping others to fulfill their needs to love and belong.**

Value Added Attachments:

Throughout the span or your life, there will be so many influential people that come and go. You will have many groups of friends and intimate connections, but only a select few get to go the distance with you in regard to friends and presumably only one spouse will make the cut. I look back on my primary/secondary school and undergrad friendships that I made, and I realize that I only have a handful of friends from all of those years and stages.

I have three really good friends that I made during high school and one that I made during my first real job, right after my undergrad. After all the contacts that I have made during my first 42 years, I have only been able to really call few individuals my friends. With this holding true for my friends, imagine how much tougher it would be to find a life partner, as I feel as though it is literally the biggest/most difficult choice that anyone can make.

When I think about my wife and how we came to be, I remember the 6 whole weeks we dated before we got married. Yes, 6 weeks, and I still don't understand what took so long. With my wife, I just knew that she was the one that I wanted to be with after only a few weeks of dating. I told myself that she was the only person that I had ever met that I wanted to take care of.

By taking that stance, it meant that I was going to be less selfish from that moment on and I was going to make her my universe. Meeting the right person certainly changed my life, but I do think that there needs to be more of an emphasis of having difficult or uncomfortable discussions before you tie the knot. The person that you decide to marry is going to be at the forefront of your life. You are going to share everything and more importantly, you will more than likely start a family with this person. As a quick aside, these uncomfortable discussions don't mean that you hate or despise anything about the other person, **we just need to relearn how to have civil conversations about difficult topics.** Step one is awareness and step two is partaking.

I feel that many couples today don't have a deep enough understanding of core values of their future partners. In the beginning, everything is great with rose colored glasses. At some point the goodness might not wear off exactly, but things will begin to get more and more complicated. According to Scott Galloway, NYU professor and author of, "The Algebra of Happiness", he mentioned before marriage proceeds, there needs to be a direct and borderline confrontational discussion about money and how both parties plan on raising children.

Half of the marriages that start today are predicted to end up in divorce, which means that in order to move forward, half of the assets must be redistributed, and everyone's lives will change. It is also important to note that most marriages are heavily impacted by money, hence the importance of having discussions about money before you settle down. I know it seems a bit out there to expect two lovebirds to ask each other point blank how old they want to be when they retire and to see the contents of each other's stock portfolios.

What I am suggesting is to have real and pragmatic conversations that will help in the immediate as well as long term time frames. Concepts like, **"who will be responsible for the financial security?"**. **"Are both parents looking to be equal providers?"**. If not, **"is everyone going to be content with their role?"**

Ultimately questions that may seem unimportant during the dating process, may save your marriage one day. Divorce can be devastating on a family from economic hardships to changing family dynamics. In my youth I had friends that seemingly overnight, went from living their best lives with toys and second homes, to uprooting all they knew and were then needed to be shuttled back and forth between two residences. It was obviously intense going from familiarity and comfortable, to being the new kid in school, on the block and on the team. This came to be, due to a buddy of mines mom, who was working on her second marriage before her first marriage had ended, thus resulting in all parties being drastically affected.

The financial impact alone was devastating, let alone the reinvention that everyone in their family went through. Also, they had the impact of stepparents on their lives and found themselves in a constant battle between what they were used to vs. how they needed to adapt to their current situation.

At the end of the day, this leads to the point of making sure that all bases are covered and you are 100% in with your partner when you get married, as so many things are banking on your success.

**One of the truest wastes of time,
Is having an inauthentic state of mind!**

In my experience, there are three types of marriages and I will let you decide what kind of marriage you want to have. First group of married couples, I call the **score keepers.** These couples look at everything as a competition. This can include how they provide, how they are with each other and possibly most important, how they parent. Score keepers have a tough time having the right intentions for the things they do.

The second grouping I view as the **broken scales.** The broken scales include a relationship where one of the partners is constantly the one under fire, succumbing to the others wants and/or being utterly dominated. When we spoke in Chapter 2 of a $100 bill, this is a key example of this scenario. There is no **partnership equivalence**, and this relationship is in danger of insecurity from one partner and the other will take it for granted.

Lastly, and frankly the grouping I strive for is the **promoters.** Promoters are constantly striving to give more and more of themselves in order to do whatever is wanted/needed for a successful marriage. They strive to be more relatable, more empathetic and more transparent. This group not only understand how important it is to strive for a successful marriage, but they also work towards creating a safe and sustainable environment for reciprocity for all they do.

Spoiler alert, being a promoter is the way to a successful marriage, it is not competing for the affection of children or trying to outperform your spouse professionally. It is also not taking an unhealthy approach to controlling your partner with manipulation or conditioning. Reciprocated love, affection, gratitude, and growth allows you to realize what was discussed in your vows! **Build each other up!**

I look at my marriage and all the trials and successes that have taken place. The only reason that I was able to get through the hard times and come out on top was the support of my wife and kids. With their love and support I was able to risk more and be more confident in situations that may have been out of my depth. Knowing deep down that no matter what happens, I have a loving family that I can confide in and come home too, as their love is unconditional. **Look to practice difficult conversations, leading to being more comfortable with being uncomfortable.**

Another key component that leads to successful is the understanding of your attachment style as well as the attachment styles of your significant other. Attachment styles have been around for 40+ years and encapsulate the relationships that were formed as children and how they now impact our adult connections. **There are 4 attachment styles as theorized by Mary Ainsworth and John Bowlby: secure, ambivalent, avoidant and disorganized.**

Secure attachment style discusses children who are typically upset when their caregivers leave, but are easily soothed when they return. They seek comfort from their parents when strangers are around and when frightened. Clear preference and trust for the primary caregiver over strangers as this behavior has been reinforced. As adults, secure attachment leads to trusting and sustainable relationships. These adults have higher self-esteem and are more empathetic.

Ambivalent attachment styles in children are displayed as children who are deeply upset when caregivers leave, but don't show comfort when they return. These children are very skeptical of strangers and may even show aggression towards parents. The children are anxious because their caregiver's availability is not consistent. As adults, this may translate into reluctance of becoming close to others and being vulnerable. Heightened feelings of inadequacy and insecurity can follow relationships and could have a difficult time moving on from a breakup or end of a relationship. Signs of smothering, possessiveness and being emotionally demanding are paramount.

Avoidant attachment style in children presents itself as a reluctance to engage with parent or caregivers. There may not be a rejection of attention from a caregiver, but there may also not be desire for affection. The child may lash out as a way to express low self-esteem and lack of attachment. As adults, this could lead to problems with intimacy and a lack of going all in emotionally with relationships. This could also lead to a desire to withhold emotions, thoughts or feelings with others while using excuses. Intimacy can also be withheld by using excuses such as working too hard or being too tired, thus leading to them rarely finding true love. A lack of empathy is also a concern of avoidant attachment.

Lastly, **disorganized** attachment in children can manifest as a combination of avoidance or resistance to caregivers. This is typically led by inconsistent parental behavior, as they display signs of reassurance and fear, leading to the child being comforted as well as frightened. As adults, they typically are afraid of intimacy and are unpredictable in relationships. These adults typically have difficulty regulating emotions and can suffer from low self-esteem. Can also be abusive and neglectful.

It is important to understand your own attachment style as well as that of your significant other. Here is a great assessment with plenty of information at no cost: attachmentproject.com. Lots of valuable information and they will email additional information if desired.

I do get asked often of how one style can work with another. I often say, don't get hung up on labels, if you are disorganized and your partner is ambivalent, start with being authentic with your partner and let them know what sets you off or how you react in situations. Once you have leveled the playing field, ask your partner to do the same. These labels are important; however, it is more important to be up front and real with your partner for a sustainable relationship.

The blessings and growth experienced by having a solid marital foundation has impacted my life in so many ways as I now understand the value of this as it leads us to develop self-esteem, self-confidence and growth, which will be discussed further in Chapters 4 and 5. A key takeaway from this section is think of your marriage as a fire. In the beginning, it can be hot, but to end up growing together, the fire needs to keep you both warm, and that means developing transparency and authenticity with each other. Your transparency and authenticity need to be fanned and fueled in order to keep going. If this does not happen, the fire will begin to fade and your relationship will slowly cool.

Reflect Recognition:

Those who read this must be in the right headspace in order to make the messages their own. I truly feel that we are far more open to accept help and praise when we seemingly don't need it. This irony is a tough way to get ahead, as when things are at their worst, we increase our inward turn.

As outsiders trying to help, these situations are hard to combat as it is hard to read the situation accurately as we don't want to overstep or seem disingenuous. After years of experience with this concept, I have come to the realize that expectations rule most things.

As we discussed in Chapter 2, expectations are extremely important in how we process new information and relationships. As displayed on the cover of this book, if we can change our view, then we are able to change our vision. **The awareness about expectations is the first step in order to change our view**, and if we can coach people what to expect from us and when, there will be no issues when we try to help in a situation that actually warrants it. When we are always in a place of trying to help and to make everyone better, then it will not be a surprise when it is necessary. I view this is as **conscious contribution.**

Conscious contribution within relationships helps to carve out the real commitment to reciprocity in others. Adam Grant made a great point in his book, "Give and Take", as **the path to our own success lies in helping others.** If we bring back the same vase that we discussed in Chapter 2, we will use the same rationale about success meaning that we are not removing sand from one of the vases and placing it in the others, conscious contribution suggests that we add more sand to both!

Of course, there is the potential fallout of getting frustrated or our feelings hurt if the individuals don't react in a way that validates and reinforces our rationale behind helping. This can also be an issue if we are not acting in a selfless and charitable manner. Every time we reach out to help someone it needs to not be for extrinsic motivation. If we are currently doing this, it can be changed if we can work on our mindset and our view of the situation. We will cover this more in Chapter 5, as this is designed to be more of an eye opener.

At different points in our lives we will need different things. You may need more outside help early and late in life, conversely you may be able to help others more in the middle years. Awareness is the key to understand where you are presently and what needs accompany that time frame.

In yet another amazing publication from Shawn Achor, "Big Potential", he talks about how there are three different types of relationships you can have and are classified as pillars, bridges and extenders. These levels of relationships fit in perfectly with what we are looking to accomplish with this book, as it goes from foundational relationship, to deepening your network, to finally weaving your way outside of your comfort zone and growing your network.

When we look at **pillars**, we ultimately view these as the needs-based relationships that allow us to feel comfortable in our current skin or role and allow us to continue to climb the pyramid of relationship needs. Pillars are valuable to maintain the status quo and to provide the unconditional support and love that we need in order to even consider moving up the pyramid.

When we look at **bridges**, these are the relationships or individuals who are outside of the pillars, yet we have faith in the security and stability of their motives. They may be able to introduce us to contacts that we wouldn't have been able to meet without their buy in or validation. They could also be individuals who have a network outside of our own, even if the demographics are similar. It may be viewed as somewhat of a parallel community.

Extenders according to Achor, are great mechanisms that help to build productive relationships, that take us out of our comfort zones. This is kind of a yin to someone else's yang. This is a great tool coupled with awareness of shortfalls, that help to make the right connections. Keep in mind that social media *hollowers* (fake followers) would not fall into this category, however they may land in the next one.

In our current landscape I feel that there is one more category that needs to be discussed, and this one is not as positive. The final category is **Tourists.** Tourists are the contacts that are presumably just taking up space in our lives or social media feeds. This attitude of passing through shows a lack of appreciation for your environment and values, and they will more than likely treat it as such. Think of them as you would, someone driving a rental car vs their own vehicle. There will certainly be a different approach to how aggressive they drive in both scenarios.

Although we are not sure of the potential, keep these tourists at arm's length emotionally in order to fully align the expectations with the outcome. Understand why they are there and that there is more than likely no tangible benefit to your connectedness.

All of these tools are only part of the story. We need to understand the fact that along with our physiological and safety needs, productive and balanced relationships are necessary in order to continue to climb towards growth. We must seek out individuals that not only help us, but will allow help to keep the cycle moving forward.

An activity I like to do with this is to have clients/students identify three individuals who fall into each of the four categories. There can be no duplication and there can be no pillars, bridges or extenders within the tourist category. The goal here is to try to understand how social media can limit our positive relationships and although we may be lured by that category, it is not sustainable, unpredictable and inconsistent.

We must be able to view our relationships with others as independent of our own and to embrace the fact that we truly don't know what they are going through. If we can create some sort of **positive pushing model**, where we assert a conscious effort to help others in a realistic, charitable and consistent manner, we will begin to see great things differently; as the view of others, social dynamics and how we view ourselves, will be positively changed!

Keep in mind that sustainable relationships require reflective work, and it is a choice. I *choose* to work for what I have. I *choose* to work for what I want!

Extreme Feats of Kindness:

There has been much discussion in my life about how to perpetuate random acts of kindness. I used to think to myself, how in the world can we make any type of real change if our actions are random? Does this mean that we think we are good people if we simply stroll about and make a uniquely good choice to help someone when the opportunity arises? **The answer is yes and please keep it up!**

I am simply looking for a better more sustained way to impact people to help with creating better habits and behaviors. The outside world is full of negative information and I know from personal experiences it can be consuming. We need to take an assertive approach to stop the negativity. At some point there was a serious disconnect between what is expected of human beings thus transitioning to dramatic and controversial content, just because it sells more advertisements on TV or in the newspapers.

We have got to be in a place where we seek out positivity and goodness in our lives in order to change how we view the landscape in order to create long lasting behavioral changes. So, what better way than to create **extreme feats of kindness?** Obviously, this is going to be subjective, as my definition of what is helpful may differ from yours. At the end of the day, if we think that we are being selfless, then if nothing else, we have improved. The only person that we have to hold us accountable is us, and honestly that can be very hard.

Our minds have a way of rejecting things that are not realistic. We have briefly touched on this already and will discuss in further detail in Chapter 5 with the Feelings Forecast, but the concept holds true in any situation, whereas we are trying to create some sort of change. With any change, whether it be diet, bedtime, positivity, etc., our body automatically goes into survival mode and reacts accordingly.

Our subconscious is always on the top of its game and there are no shortcuts to changing habits and being a different person. It took years and years to be who you are, do you think that your mind is going to give it up, especially as you have survived to this point? There must be true intrinsic motivation and authentic desire to make changes in order for anything to be sustained. It takes work and discipline, but in the end, I know you will be better off for it.

If we look at a book by Josh Kauffman called, "The First 20 Hours", he explains that the traditional time frame of mastering a new skill is at 10,000 hours, however if you want to learn something at a basic level it only takes 20 hours. Ok, that sounds far less overwhelming and maybe even attainable. **That about forty-five minutes a day for a month to focus on something new.** This is where it starts, we have to make a conscious effort to invest the time in ourselves to make a real change. The amazing part of this is that you can take the "two birds" approach.

For example, today I wanted to incorporate spending time with my son and also work on my kindness skills. So, I sat outside and watched him pogo stick for well over an hour. I was able to give him the attention that he needs for his development, while simultaneously working on being kind and charitable. There is nothing wrong with getting something back when you are kind, in fact it usually helps me to continue in those behaviors. It is all about awareness and how to develop into the person you want to be.

As this book was written as more of an abstract way to understand psychological concepts, I tried to make my existential experiences applicable to most situations. **Please don't hesitate from looking at one example and seeing if it will work for a situation specific to your life.** Transferability is tolerated and more than likely it will. It will take a conscious effort to make the change, however the fact that you are reading this book means you are ready.

Another example of a way to incorporate kindness feats, (I say feats as it is certainly an accomplishment and not just a checked box) is that typically for Christmas my wife and I discuss gifts and what to give our children for the holiday. We have a process that has worked for a few years and it goes like this, you get something you want, something you need, something to wear and something to read.

The rub here is that my kids don't need anything and I tell them this, so our families "need" gift goes in the form of a donation to our church. The only reason I am telling you this, is that it would be so much easier to shower my kids with gifts on Christmas morning and see their little faces light up with cheer. But what good is that in the long run?

With this extreme feat of kindness, my children are growing up knowing that the world does not revolve around them and that they are pretty lucky to have the things that they do. It is all about how you view your surroundings and having awareness.

Another way to view this is to look at it as proactive vs reactive. Extreme feats vs random acts. Here are some examples of Extreme Feats of Kindness that go from easy to requiring slightly more preparation. It just takes the will and desire to create your own opportunities to help. Start small and grow at your comfort level. Keep in mind that the more you are willing to help others, it will simultaneously benefit your fulfillment and joy levels. No wrong answers here!

Examples of Extreme Feats of Kindness (easy to hard and lots of room for things in between):

- Give money (transactional, can always make more)
- SMILE and SAY HI to people you don't know!!
- Helping an elderly person cross the street
- Paying for service members lunch
- Give an unsolicited compliment to someone.
- Be **vulnerable** enough to ask someone if **they** need help.
- Give back to nature
- **GIVE YOUR TIME FREELY (non-renewable resource, greatest feat)**

An old Buddhist saying states: the biggest mistake we make in life is thinking we have TIME. You don't own time, but you spend it and its simultaneously free and priceless.

When you change your outlook by doing this more it becomes easier and easier for you to continue. It's a muscle you have to continually work out so start and maintain the great work. An exercise I like to do with my students is to have them write down 10 things that they feel are possible to complete in regards to charitable acts. Once done I have them rank them from most to least likely. Everyone is different and this gets them thinking about how to execute vs seeing it as a hurdle.

Do you want to be better or do you want your previous habits to be so grand that they suffocate your goals and progression? You can view your world in a better light, you just have to try to shine in the shade!

The quickest way to mental health is to make yourself available to someone else!

Perpetuation of Real-Life Interactions:

As we grow more and more fond of our devices, it seems as though we have an emotional attachment to them. As I mentioned before, our devices help us find the nearest gas station and order us new jeans when we need them. It is pretty much the best friend we never had. However, there is a flip side to this, as with everything else in this book, the individuals who program the content for your phone now know your tendencies and wants, and they exploit it.

Those lines of code now know what will keep you looking at your phone longer as they know what you want to view. This emotional attachment can lead down a rabbit hole of fake news or any other types of grooming behaviors, because it knows that you will continue to trust the content and not sever the relationship. So how do we break the cycle and how do we cultivate more real-life interactions? The answer to this is to simply seek them out, be aware of the fact that we are on our devices way too much and last but not least, understand that we act differently in real life situations vs. artificial ones.

Here are two situations, and in both scenarios, you are on your way home from work and would love to get there as safe and as quick as possible. Imagine you are driving in your car along the highway. You are in the middle lane, beginning to merge to the right to eventually get off the freeway. It is late in the afternoon, so traffic is mounting, however you are still traveling at your desired rate of speed. You end up merging to the far right and traffic is now backing up, as many travelers are attempting to get off the freeway. You are now in the off ramp and traffic is stopped. While you are waiting patiently to begin moving again, a car comes up right next to you, has their blinker on and is nudging their way in front of you, somewhat forcefully. Let's stop right there and move directly into the second scenario.

The second scenario is you are heading into the grocery store to pick up a few things for dinner tonight. You grab ten items or so, to move into the fast checkout lane. Again, you are waiting patiently for your turn in line and someone walks up to you and asks if they can sneak in front as they are in a hurry and they only have milk and eggs. Let's stop there and evaluate both scenarios.

The first scenario, you are driving and someone is trying to merge in front of you on the off ramp and the second scenario someone is trying to get in front of you in the checkout line of the grocery store. Which one of these scenarios are you more likely to comply with, the car merger or the grocery cutter?

I can tell you that the decision you probably made is that you are more likely to let the grocery cutter move in front of you in line. But why would you allow this and not the car merger? **Being detached from scenarios allow us to be less human and more confrontational. Interaction is where oxytocin is released, and it allows us to feel more alive and ultimately more human!**

When we are driving in the car, we are safe in our vehicle and we know that the decisions we make will only affect us for the next few seconds. The rate of speed is too fast and cars are too maneuverable to have to actually be accountable and deal with issues we experience.

On the flip side of this, while we are waiting in lines or surrounded by other people, we are far more attached and have to take a much different approach. We become humans again and the best comes out in us. We strive to help and we show empathy and can relate to people. We are forced to slow down and when that happens, we are transformed. We put ourselves in other people's shoes, we can seek out opportunities to connect and to help. Those are things that don't take place when we are flying by at 70mph and we have little to no awareness of who or what surrounds us.

Happiness only real when shared

-Chris McCandless, Into the Wild

In an enlightening book by Dr. David Eagleman called, "Livewired", he discusses the importance of cognitive challenges and discusses the value of real-life interactions. He speaks to the value of working and living with individuals, and how the uncertainty and real time problem solving that other people bring, can help with the building of new neural roadways and bridges. Ultimately, dealing with other people is one of the best ways to maintain a healthy brain.

The more we can limit detaching ourselves from situations, the better we will be with real life interacting, as this awareness is what is needed to make a behavioral change. So, if we take this train of thought to how it relates to technology, we need to understand that social media and technology is not real. We are not the same people on and off our phones.

Another great resource is a Ted Talk by Professor David Amadio and he talks about the difference in concentrations of sought-after vs raw dopamine. He talks about not settling for a manufactured release of a fraction of a normal dose of dopamine by searching for it in social media. When it is natural and comes to you it is far more intense. This idea comes back to modulating the flow of information (previously discussed). Control what information you see and consume, don't give anyone else that power. The benefits of real-life interactions are a way to get this real dose!

An example of this is I have my class speak with their peers about an upcoming holiday for a few minutes. I ask them to include everyone at their table and really dive in with an intimate conversation.

Then I ask them to pull out their phones and text two people to inquire about their plans for the same upcoming holiday. Preferably they reach out to people they haven't spoken to in a few weeks. Once done, I ask them to write down the difference in feelings. Almost every time there is a less joyous state of mind being displayed from texting, vs the real human connection.

This is why we have internet trolls and e-ballers, because the detachment empowers specific behaviors in people that they wouldn't have otherwise had. Computer programmers know what will keep you glued to your phones and they seek out ways to make you feel comfortable with things you probably wouldn't discuss in real life conversations.

It is so very important to be aware of the person you are when you are detached from other living beings and the person you are when around others, especially when you are around loved ones within your social circle. Notice how you feel and how you adapt when face to face with others. Seek to replicate that state of being, in as many situations as possible.

There was a study in 1956 by Harry Harlow whereas he removed an infant monkey and placed it with two surrogate mothers. One of the mothers had a unlifelike face, was comprised of wire and was able to deliver milk on demand. The other surrogate mother, had a realistic face and was soft and comforting. Over the course of the experiment, the monkey strongly preferred the cloth monkey over the one bearing food and what was really profound was that in the presence of the cloth mother, the monkey was more curious, and showed far more interest in exploring the room. Once the cloth surrogate was removed, the monkey froze, cried and seemed utterly lost without the cloth surrogate being there.

I couldn't help but take from this that in life, the workplace, relationships, our primitive nature is dead on. We need connection, security and attachment far more than any extrinsic rewards. Whether its milk or a paycheck, that cannot be replicated or substituted for an oxytocin filled, reality based real time connection. Keep this in mind as you seek out fulfillment and joy, as the path may or may not lead your where you truly WANT to go!

Summary:

- Strength in love and belonging starts with family relationships in the home.
- We must have a strong sense of love and belonging in order to set ourselves up for self-confidence and growth throughout our lives.
- Value of forgiveness.
- Technology can be valuable in regard to providing a mechanism to be more present in the home.
- Your spouse is the most important relationship you can have.
- It is important to have the uncomfortable questions and understanding of expectations before you get married.
- The highest ceiling of self-confidence and potential occurs as you have a solid familial baseline.
- Understanding and/or manufacturing expectations can help in social settings.
- Awareness of different types of marriages.
- Understand your attachment style.

- Conscious contribution will help to achieve and maintain personal and group success.
- Understand relationship needs and where your network ranks (pillar, bridge, extender or tourist) and how to maximize your network.
- Behavioral change starts with awareness and slight habitual change. Start to see the world differently when seeking to find ways to help others.
- Find a quantifiable way to work in behavioral change to your life.
- What type of charity has the highest value?
- Helping others can be charitable while also benefitting you. Look for ways to maximize both.
- View your universe in the way that you want it to look.
- Look for and be aware of opportunities to have real life interaction and follow behaviors that lead to more.
- Detach from fake and attach to real.

- Understand the layers of value with real life interactions.

- Oxytocin helps to feel more human, seek out opportunities to release it more!

- Seek real Dopamine!

- Familiarize yourself with seeking out opportunities to connect.

Chapter 4

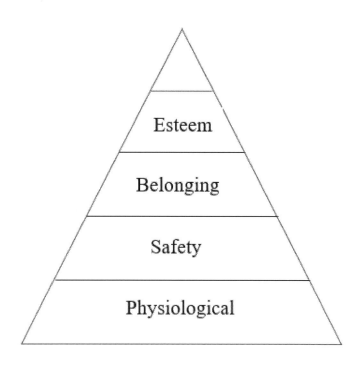

When esteem needs are brought up, I go right to the creation and maintenance of things like: self-confidence, self-esteem, respect for self and an overall sense of accomplishment in various aspects of our lives. However, as we have said in previous chapters, what is missing and/or how can this list be improved upon?

- **Embrace your story**
- **Mindset**
- **Don't be so Hard on Yourself**
- **Psychological Capital**
- **Relive Recent Accomplishments**

When moving through the rest of this chapter and looking at the sections above, we will formulate a better understanding of our own unique and individual story, how they come to be and why they matter. Next, we will look deeper at our mindset and how this awareness can allow us to advance ourselves while creating sustainable change with newly developed habits. We will also discuss how handicapping shame takes place and will discuss some ways to combat it. We will then look at some key characteristics of self-confidence within the Psychological Capital Theory, as well as going over other components in order to provide a more holistic approach to esteem. To wrap up the chapter we will discuss how important it is to relive past success as a vehicle in order to help propel current and future successes.

Confident Discernment

"A man cannot be comfortable without his own approval"
-Mark Twain

Embrace your Story:

The year 2020 will certainly go down in the history books as being a year to remember (or forget, your call). But despite all of the drawbacks, challenges and trials that have shown up during the past year, we still need to understand the value that all these experiences bring to our individual story.

During one of our walks, my wife Myken brought up the fact that people keep saying the word, "should". They say the things should be this way or that way, instead of embracing what is actually taking place. To pull forward some of the components of, "Feelings Forecast", "should", is not part of your circumstance, however it is a way your brain views what you think your world "should" be.

Some of the discussions I have heard are:

- My son should have been able to receive his diploma in front of a crowd of people and have an official graduation.
- I should be able to visit my customers and do better this year.
- I should have been able to visit my family across the country/in another country.

The fact of the matter is that just like we discussed earlier in this chapter, we must be able to identify the thoughts that we wish to change and make said changes. In doing so we are able to understand the fact that your story is impenetrable and unique to you. It is YOUR STORY. What if you changed your thoughts and decided to say to yourself?

- This is so awesome, I was one of the first students to graduate via zoom, and all of my extended family, (not just my parents and siblings) were able to watch my slide on the screen and cheer me on!

- Now I can visit more customers in any given week, as I am not spending time at airports and driving!

- I can spend time on camera with my family knowing that we are all safe from any potential disease and harm!

It is all about how you think about your circumstances that can change your feelings. I like to use the stages of grief whenever there is any type of emotional struggle that needs to be thwarted. I know we discussed this earlier, however it applies here as well. The five stages of grief are: denial, anger, depression, bargaining and acceptance. I am sure that we all can agree that we have utilized this model at some point, within this past year. With the roller coaster of emotion that this year has caused, it is exceedingly difficult to organize our outside world in a way that gives us comfort.

This year has led me to understand the severity of the pandemic and prepare for the duration of time that we will need to be locked down. I have also been angry with things that were completely out of my control and was in need of thought adjustments. I was also sad and felt powerless to help my family or friends with devastating outcomes and have then moved to try and rack my brain to find unconventional solutions.

With that being said, I feel that the ability to embrace our stories allows us to get to the final stage of grief, which is acceptance. With the understanding of our circumstance and the ability to change our thoughts as needed, it allows us to find **closure** and be in charge of our emotional outcomes. Please keep this in mind as the new year progresses, and let's hope and pray that the worst is behind us.

When we look at our stories, we need to understand that we are the whole as well as a sum of the parts. When I think about conversations I had with my grandmother or even my parents, we discussed the aspects of their lives that were difficult and the shit they went through. Their stories are filled with rich history, and situations of adversity and resilience. That is the good stuff!

Also, I wanted to bring attention to the stories of the youth in our lives. So often there is little to no patience in what they are looking to accomplish. They may be looking at social media, their parents, fiends, siblings and want more than they have, that is literally unattainable at their age. **Ambition is great; however, I would suggest that they try and have more patience, grind it out and understand that the people they are comparing themselves are on a different chapter of their story.** You can be on chapter 5, but your parents are on chapter 40, social media influencers could be on chapter 12 and your siblings could be on chapter 8 or even chapter 2. Have patience, go at your speed and seek a fulfilled life.

There is an amazing story of Chris McCandless who ventured off for a "Great Alaskan Adventure", leaving all worldly norms and comforts behind him. The book/film is titled, "Into the Wild" but the majority of the story doesn't take place with Chris actually living in Alaska or the wild, the majority of the story takes place on his path to reach his goal. **There is a focus on the relationships he cultivates, the present and the journey.** So often in our lives, we are hardwired to reach a goal, that we literally miss what is around us along the way. **A great quote from John Lennon states, "Life is what happens, when you are busy making other plans".**

If we focus on the now, the real, and the connections, the destination will take care of itself!

As we look back at our lives, I am sure there are some parts that we would like to not have top of mind or even not remember at all. It is so important to understand that we are better off because of all of the: trials, successes, failures, tragedies and victories. Your story is your story, and it is the only one of its kind. Our stories are there to provide references for future decisions and offer up appreciation of where we are.

Owning our story isn't with pity. It is with strength and perseverance. It's looking at our experiences and thinking, "damn, I went through all of this and it made me better, I am the Phoenix that we discussed in the introduction!" When we pity ourselves, we aren't taking responsibility, we blame others and we will feel powerless in our stories.

This tweak in our perspective is learned and if it wasn't learned previously, we can learn it and apply it now. **You get to write your own script.** Think about writing a play for only one character. You don't get to choose the other

163

characters personalities or their decisions. You can only choose how your character acts and responds to others. Think of different ways you can write that script; then choose who, what, where, how you want your character to be.

I've read this script and the costume fit,
So I'll play my part!
Cleopatra, The Lumineers

Because you will never please everyone, some will think you are too loud or too shy. Some will think you are ugly and some will see you as attractive. You don't get to choose how others see you, so you may as well see yourself as you want to be seen. Flip the script, be empowered and change your view!

Mindset:

In this section we will cover mindset and how it can impact our motivation and success. When I think mindset, I immediately think agency. I feel that our mindset is an **absolute choice** that we make day in and day out. We will soon discuss the five (or seven) stages to the Feelings Forecast, and I feel that mindset fits in nicely with our perceptions (thoughts).

We can look at mindset in a multitude of ways. For example, we can strive to have a positive mindset where we seek out the good in the world and it is almost like we have a **positive detector**. Walking around on the streets waving this metal device around looking for situations and opportunities to be positive. This may sound a bit extreme, however I have tried to convince you in this book that we are looking to find ways to change our behavior and if we need to be a bit extreme in order to solidify the habits, then so be it.

Another interesting view on mindset is from Carol Dweck and her book, **"Mindset, the New Psychology of Success".** Now this concept is a bit long in the tooth at this point, however the concepts are fantastic! Basically, we have two ways of looking at our perception of the world, "fixed" and "growth".

If we look at the "fixed" mindset mentality, it explains just that. Everything in our lives in terms of motivation and characteristics are static and unable to change. Some examples of this could be:

- **I am already good enough.**
- **I am the prettiest girl here.**
- **My parents think I am the best player.**
- **I don't need to learn new things.**
- **Your opinion is less important than mine.**

When you say things like the bottom two during your development you tend to rest on your laurels a bit and quit trying to achieve. After all, you have already achieved success so why put forth more effort?

Has anyone ever known someone who was exceptional at a sport or a subject in middle or high school, only to flame out and be merely average at it later on? I can think of so many people in high school that were in the popular crowd, or were put on such a pedestal due to abilities they had at an early age, and got stuck thinking that they needn't improve or that they are better than those whom they are competing with, all the while they are not trying to be the best version of themselves. Maybe they were unhappy in a job, yet made excuses on why they couldn't do better? Made a lot of excuses and ultimately played the victim card? Gets in fights with people and it is always the other persons fault? All of these tendencies are that of the fixed mindset as those individuals are trapped in the compare and compete mode.

The issue here is that they stopped trying! They stopped trying to develop skills and characteristics to enhance themselves, because they were constantly getting spoon fed the notion that were amazing and already the best. If someone told me that I was the best at anything, where would my motivation be? Why would I continue to try? The issue with a "fixed" mindset, is that it leaves you with nowhere to go.

Now let's focus on a "growth" mindset. Now this mindset looks to perpetuate effort and leaves the individuals thinking that the focus is on improvement. Some examples could be:

- **I don't know everything and that is OK.**
- **I can learn from others.**
- **I will never stop trying.**
- **My potential is unknown.**
- **I can achieve anything I put my mind to.**

These phrases fall way more in line with the message of this book. We are capable of many things, as long as we are aware of our shortcomings, and we have the know-how and desire to create change in our lives. A focus of this book is to perpetuate the ability to create positive change and this is one of the best levers to get there.

We can use growth motivators like the following to determine how we perceive ourselves and our growth:

- **I can be happy for others when they have success.**
- **We can look inward for ways to improve, whilst being receptive of feedback when it is warranted.**
- **We can embrace failure as a temporary mechanism to improvement.**
- **We do need to understand that skillsets are developed, not inherited.**
- **A positive attitude and solid work ethic can start us on a path to growth.**
- **I can change my lens to reflect the positive in the world and if I do so, I understand that this action could change my vision.**

To quickly rehash, our mindsets are a culmination of years of development and choices we have made along the way. These experiences have defined our upbringing and allow us to be unique. There may come a time however, that we understand that some things have run their course and it

169

is time for a change, this is where a mindset change comes in.

The brain does its best to limit newness. Again, it says if we are surviving, we are good, and anything that seems hard from a biological, social, psychological and physiological standpoint, is probably right. Don't be a knucklehead, but try new things.

Another interesting concept is from Angela Duckworth, as she looks deeper into **Grit**. Grit looks deeper at finding a way to develop something you're interested in and continue to get better at it. Despite hard and possibly unnecessary work/progress. Identify key individuals in your life that have grit. They can have grit in anything, as those traits are extremely transferable. Don't forget you are the sum of the 5 people you hang out with the most. Might as well find people who are high in Grit.

Change the way you look at situations in your life. Try to learn, grow and develop as much as possible. Keep the mindset open, allowing your lens to continually be refreshed!

Don't be so hard on yourself:

I know so many people who don't give themselves any kind of breaks. They are constantly ridiculing and doubting their choices and behaviors. There is a ton of buzz in the air about how being vulnerable is the best way toward growth being courageous. But what happens when we decide to put ourselves out there and give it our best shot only to fail or fall on our faces?

I have been there many times and I would assume that many of you have as well. So, what is the magic bullet to prepare for and/or deal with the dark side of shame? It may be better to point out a few things that I have learned along the way. I often wondered what the difference between guilt and shame is, as they seem very similar. **Brené Brown stated in her book, "Dare to Lead", that guilt is more of a label of an action and shame is a direct attack on your worthiness. For example, she stated that guilt is saying that I did something bad vs. shame saying that I am bad. Pretty big difference there!**

The reason that I felt it is important to include this section of the chapter is to find a way past the destructive behaviors and thoughts associated with shame and to show you the way out. From personal experience, there have been

171

times that I have been so upset and so hopeless that I didn't know how I was going to pull out of it. Times like these are filled with physiological responses like panic attacks and isolation. Basically, horrible scenarios that I can't foresee a resolution.

I always tell my wife that I have a pretty good grasp on things if I can wrap my head around them, understand why they happened and/or to dissect the motivation of others. When I can't figure out why certain difficult things were put in my way, I can't help but feel tremendous amounts of humiliation and embarrassment. These could take the form of faith-based trials or simply new challenges that force a new outlook.

Some questions that I have asked myself are: Why would I have such a hard time providing? Why are my children so challenging and why can't they make friends? Why is it my sales territory that gets crushed during the pandemic and I am unable to recover? Why as a man and a father, do I feel sad and down, I can't remember my father feeling this way? Why do I look and feel so old, I am not ready for this? Why, why, why?

When we look at these things with compassion, curiosity and creativity, we may be able to more

thoroughly understand our actions and silo our own healing.

**Mind full of questions and a
Teacher in my soul, so it goes.**

Guaranteed, Eddie Vedder

The crazy thing about these situations and when I felt shame, is that the awareness acted as a springboard to move me forward and this is when I was able to transform my life and do amazing things! For me, feeling this type of shame was the birthplace of the most incredible things in my life. If you look back to Chapter 1 when we talked about how the cravings in your life suffocate all the good and take over, just know that shame is the same! Shame will swoop in and take over your dirty consciousness and limit your ability to reach your goals and potential.

We have discussed in this book the power of awareness and the same holds true for shame. If you are aware of feeling shame, the worst thing you can do is to go down in a deep dark hole, no matter how appealing that may be at the time. Shame hates empathy, so if you can try to reach out to people you trust and express your feelings, empathy can take over and help the recovery process.

The people that truly know you will be keenly aware of something being off with you and will reach out and try to be there for you. Just let them! **Empathy is the enemy of shame, as there is no way for shame to persevere with the power of human connection looking over you.** However, like everything else in this book, empathy needs to be learned and the only way to learn it is to understand the value and seek out opportunities to be empathetic with others. As a quick aside, make sure you are also aware of false validation of shameful thoughts, as these can prove immobilizing. False validation can come in the form of a close friend simply agreeing with you in order to make you happy, when they should take a more objective approach if your view is flawed.

Let people know you are there for them on a regular basis. Let loved ones know that you are well aware of mistakes they may make or their shortcomings, but you love them anyway (possibly due to their lack of perfection). One of my favorite sayings is, **"the beauty is in the flaws".**

An assessment I feel is very important for understanding how we can love and be loved in the most efficient manner is to understand our love language **(5lovelanguages.com),** as well as the love language of our romantic partner, close friends, parents or children. There are 5 love languages and these hold an impact far beyond our romantic interests. It can transfer or overlap with professionalism, motivation and personality. The 5 languages are: Quality Time, Physical Touch, Receiving Gifts, Words of Affirmation and Acts of Service.

Quality time can be viewed as just taking the time to be with your partner, literally over quantity of time. Paying attention to what matters to them and offering the most valuable resource we have to them. **Physical touch** is not just sexual, it can be looked at as appropriate ways to connect and can lead to secure attachment. **Gifts** are important as they are a literal gift, but it also shows the though behind the gift as well as a sacrifice made in order to provide it. **Words of affirmation** can be viewed as more important than actions. This can be great when uttering praise or validation, but can also be destructive if not chosen correctly. Lastly, **acts of service** can be an unsolicited vacuuming session or washing your partners car before they leave in the morning. Just something that shows them you appreciate, choose and value them is what makes this work.

It is also important to understand that flaws and imperfections are what make us unique, they are what makes us Us. Those are not wrinkles on your brow, they are lines that make up the story of how you got here. Those are not extra pounds around your midsection, they are a map of where you have been.

I think too often we look at the people around us and think that they have it so easy or they have it made, when we have no friggin idea about their story. If we are indeed looking to become more empathetic, we must try and identify opportunities to deeply connect with others and hope that what we have done to help, will allow help for us down the road. Reciprocity is crucial for empathy to thrive.

Life is about experiencing the good with the bad. Everything can't be the way you want it to be, otherwise you would not have a barometer of what is real and possible. The counterweight is necessary for perspective. Take the time to look at your life and uncover/identify blessings and not what you lack.

Carl Rogers came up with a theory on, "Self-Concept", whereas he would ask questions like, "who are you", in order for you to reveal your top-of-mind emotion. He also discussed the push and pull between the ,"**Real**" and "**Ideal**" self. Ideal self being the person you would like to be, and self being the person you are.

You Think that You Can Front When Revelation Comes?

So What'cha Want, Beastie Boys

It's all about how you view your world, through what lens and understanding if you have the awareness of your owner's manual. For example: Don't look at getting older as bad just because you are not as athletic as you once were or maybe your looks are fading. Look at getting older as a way to be wiser and more experienced. You may be able to become a grandparent. The possibilities are endless, because you are afforded opportunities. Also, don't forget that not everyone is afforded the luxury of getting old, don't take it for granted.

When we look at the importance of the linear fashion of the hierarchy of needs, as we have discussed in this book, we first have physiological needs, once those are met, we move to safety, then on to love and belonging. Without the first 3 tiers being attained sequentially, shame would run rampant and have no competition. Meeting the needs presented in the third chapter of this book equip us against shame and allow us to not only fight, but to prevail.

177

Psychological Capital:

When I think about self-confidence or esteem, there are a few characteristics that I feel are the most important. In his book, "Psychological Capital", Fred Luthans identified four key characteristics that encompass what is going right with individuals as opposed to deficiency-based definitions. The characteristics described in this theory fit in perfectly with how I regard self-confidence on the path to growth.

Other similar definitions of capital could include social capital, which involves the strength of your network and could include social status (indirectly covered in Chapter 3). We also have financial capital, which includes your portfolio, income and overall wealth (which was covered in Chapter 2). Ideological capital, which thrives on the strength of creativity, ideas and moral compass (which we will be going over in Chapter 5).

Psychological Capital is defined as **an individual's positive psychological state of development**, while covering 4-character components that lead to growth. The four components are: hope, which is the motivating or redirecting of our plans in order to attain success. The second component is efficacy, which is understanding what is being asked and is equipped to put in the necessary effort for

178

completion. The third component of Psychological Capital is resilience, which is comprised of bouncing back despite adversity and still achieving the desired result. Lastly, the fourth component is optimism, where individuals have a positive disposition toward future challenges and goals.

Why I feel that this theory is important as we discuss self-confidence is the four components together help to reinforce aspects of self-confidence that they wouldn't be able to do on their own. When all four are together, positive potential is realized.

Individuals that have high levels of **hope** have the necessary willpower to change, problem solve and uncover multiple solutions. Change is a very real issue with self-esteem, and with the implementation of hope, herein lies the ability to change and alternate one's pathways in time of need. **Goal setting** (which we will discuss more in Chapter 5) is paramount when developing hope, as it propels the individual's ability to set clear and concise objectives and set forth a path of achievement.

In looking again at goals, individuals with high levels of hope are far better at setting anchoring goals that help along the process of goal realization, as well as achievement of larger more elusive goals. High levels of hope also help with the development of **autonomy**, as well as **critical thinking.**

If we focus now on **efficacy,** we will notice that in many situations, whether professional or personal, we typically lean toward things that are seemingly attainable, and may shy away from more challenging or out of our arranged purview. I know we had discussed vulnerability in previous chapters, but here we are again. As previously stated, vulnerability is at the onset of change and creativity.

Despite things looking difficult and uncomfortable, we must again grow our mustaches with pride and confidence because we no longer are afraid of how it will be perceived. High levels of efficacy produce this type of thinking. Another thing to consider is that just because you have high levels of efficacy in one aspect of your life, say work, that doesn't mean you can't transfer that skill to your love life. It won't just happen for you automatically; you just need to show up and put yourself out there over and over again despite knowing that it's going to be tough.

A way to strengthen our self-efficacy is to better understand our **false beliefs** and look to replace them with **new experiences.** This can work in a multitude of fashions, for example if you are hung up on not being able to romantically speak to a person of interest, then you must continue to be vulnerable to put yourself in positions to safely try and create new experiences of success in order to combat the false beliefs of yourself. This can work with many facets of things in the workplace and can also help with **Imposter Syndrome,** as that is a disorder filled with false beliefs.

Resilience could be my favorite component of Psychological Capital, as I feel like this could be one of my superpowers. Not sure if it is a good thing that I have experienced lots of resilience in my life, as that means I have been down and out a bunch. However, I feel like this tool in my tool belt is now an asset.

Setbacks and adversity in regard to vulnerability and confidence are as predictable as a paycheck. Resilience is the only aspect of Psychological Capital that I feel like we cannot go out and proactively try and develop. It is certainly a byproduct of crappy situations that we had no control of. With that being said, there is still no reason why we can't harness the ability to develop resilience and use every opportunity to improve.

There are a few ways we are able to better cope with setbacks. In a TedTalk we previously discussed, "The Flip Phone Manifesto" by David Amadio, one of his suggestions for a more fulfilled life was to **make reality the default setting.** That theory applies here as well, when we are more prepared to understand how things are supposed to feel and pan out in our universe. Another great suggestion to cope with setbacks are to develop our abilities to **pivot in real time.** Things will often not go our way, but our ability to focus on something else equally beneficial will serve us in the long run.

Optimism is not just an overall outlook about good things that will happen, it also focuses on the reasoning and attributes as to why the good things will happen. Optimism takes a deeper look at things like; motivation, positive thought and realism.

Another aspect of optimism that I really like, is that individuals high in optimism show signs of high efficacy simultaneously. They are typically able to identify situations whereas they need help and are not afraid to ask for it. Most importantly, they are able to identify what is needed for future success and the ability to strive towards it.

A way to institute higher levels of optimism is to make a focused and specific effort to **reframe** stress as a challenge rather than a setback (clean and dirty stress refresher). We discussed this earlier in the book, but that awareness and fortitude will allow higher levels of this trait.

I am going into lots of details in regard to the Psychological Capital components, as I deem them crucial for this stage in the journey we are on. These four attributes show more baselines of what to expect in terms of soft skills to strive toward as well as an understanding of why they are important in regard to self-confidence.

At this point I am going to come back to the importance of creating sustainable behavioral habits that allow us to maintain and create more Psychological Capital benefits in our lives. Look for opportunities to be optimistic, hopeful, confident and resilient. These are soft skills that must be tended to and kept up, as these skills will atrophy with lack of attention.

Another major component it is necessary to discuss in this section, as it pertains to positive psychological capital is **Flow.** Flow is some sort of experience that is deemed so engaging, that it becomes worth doing for the sake of just doing it. Ultimately creating its own motor! Look for opportunities in your life for things that create their own motor and the outside world seemingly shuts down. Your flow can cause a lack of concern of the constructs of time and may lead to a sense of complete control and focus. **Being in a Flow state of mind equals clarity!**

I know this all seems like a lot to do, but it is certainly necessary and with the right outlook and approach these behaviors can be learned. The fact that you are reading this book means that you are looking for answers in some capacity, you don't know it all and you are open to suggestions. Change simply requires awareness and a purpose. If we can get there together, we are well on our way.

Relive Recent Accomplishments:

Through the course of any day, you will find that there are situations that lift you up and some that weigh you down. As we have mentioned before, this counterweight is helpful in hindsight, however when you are in a downturn, things probably look bleak.

A surefire way to up your confidence at any given time is to think back to previous successes. There is no possible way to think back to a victory and suffer a loss of self-confidence. We go through our lives experiencing so many things and experience so many outcomes. This issue is that it is exceedingly difficult to remember victories we had and all the circumstances surrounding it, while we are in the jaws of failure. It is a tough concept as when we are going through a breakup or rigorous emotional situation, we typically cover the **highlights** in our brain which covers mostly positive and fun memories in order to cope or heal, rather than going over the **documentary** which is a linear depiction of reality. In this situation, we are looking to do the same thing. Try and remember facts, feelings, hell- anything that helps us to recall a victorious time.

In thinking back to my last bout with not getting what I wanted, I remember going for a drive and leaving my support staff behind (It reminds me of when I was young and I had a stomach ache and all I had to do was to take the dam medicine that my parents were giving me). But I didn't, I just sat there stubborn and refused to take the grape goo that would help me to move on.

That is how I deal with failure, adversity, shame, you name it. My go to, is to be alone and be a man with my thoughts and figure it out on my own. We discussed how the support of key folks in our lives can help us to crush shame, but how else can we combat failure, when it doesn't live in the shame realm?

I feel that a great way to do this is to keep success top of mind by keeping a journal of all my victories no matter how small. Sometimes we are at the top of our game and when we experience a little setback, we may have enough **conquest credits** tucked away in our minds to redeem and help get us over the small hump of defeat. Other times we are struggling at a pretty strong clip and you have been in the basement in regard to performance for longer than you would like, or you are accustomed too.

The journaling helps me to read over my past successes to help me get through whatever toughness life has recently thrown me. I find it is helpful as I am able to recreate the situation in my mind to help me relive as much of it as possible. I can visualize how my wife looked at me when I got my dissertation completed or I remember my boss fighting for me in a battle that I thought was unwinnable. I remember how these situations went down, as well as how they made me feel. In a great study by Speer, Bhanji and Delgado, they stated that "Reminders of happy memories can bring back pleasant feelings tied to the original experience, suggesting an intrinsic value in reminiscing about the positive past."

Remember earlier in the book that our minds cannot determine what tense the emotion we are feeling was in. Whether or not it was past or present, our minds view it the same. So why not play the game and re-experience all the times that made us feel good and try our best to replicate?

I have realized throughout my life that when times get tough, you need to have a tool or a process in place to remember when you had a better result. Journaling can get a bit tiresome and sometimes it is hard to remember to write down how you are feeling during victory, when all you want to do is celebrate.

It goes back (again) to trying to create positive change in your life by creating improved behaviors. I have tried a few ways to journal so that it is efficient with time and effort. First, I used the notes app on my phone and began to type in what I thought was important about that situation. Shortly, I wisened up and began to use the talk to text feature on the app and just clicked the button and spoke clearly and concisely about what I wanted to remember.

The key here is to get so good at this that you barely need to write much down except some key words. For example, words like, "sparky, news and 6fig" helps me to remember a very large sale I made and I just need a few key words to bring it back to life.

I also use this tool when I think back to what I am thankful for. I try to archive a few things that I value in my life, (with little intentional duplication) on a daily basis. The same premise holds true for this. When life throws you curveballs, you have a tried and true tool in your belt that you can relive amazing parts of your life and also do a reset to highlight what really matters. **If we can cultivate a habit of looking out and thinking about things we appreciate, we slowly change our lens and do a better job with overall gratitude!**

A really good barometer of understanding our own inner faculties is to complete one of my favorite personality tests. Now this test is comprised of the Big 5 or OCEAN traits. First, it measures your imagination or **openness** to new experiences. Second, it looks at **conscientiousness** and your ability to regulate immediate gratification. Third, it moves to discuss where you recharge your batteries and the value you put on social connection with **extraversion**. Next, it moves to cooperation, loyalty and **agreeableness**. Finally, it looks at emotional instability, anxiety and **neuroticism**. If you have a few minutes, I would highly recommend taking this test to better understand your emotional baselines.

www.truity.com

"Not until we are lost, do we begin to find ourselves"
-Henry David Thoreau

Summary:

- Circumstances cannot change; however, our thoughts can impact how we feel about our stories.
- Stay away from the word, "should" as it suggests an alternate reality.
- Embracing our story allows us to find acceptance and closure.
- Flip the script, be empowered and change your view!
- Mindsets are a choice.
- Have the "fixed" vs "growth" mindset battle in your mind.
- Constantly be looking for opportunities to grow.
- Create your own result.
- Understand how to move from dirty to clean discomfort and how you can differentiate.
- Difference between guilt and shame. Guilt goes after behaviors and shame goes after worthiness.
- Empathy is the enemy of shame.

- Be on the lookout for increased opportunities to be empathetic.
- Psychological Capital as a whole, can lead to success and goal attainment
- Hope covers motivating or redirecting towards success.
- Efficacy is a thorough understanding of expectations and follow through for action.
- Resilience shows a focus to bounce back despite failure and/or adversity.
- Optimistic individuals have a positive disposition towards challenges and goals.
- Understand a path to improvement for all Psychological Capital components.
- Keep a journal of victories, no matter how small.
- Identify key words to help you relive key situations that help overcome current adversity
- There is no growth in the comfort zone and no comfort in the growth zone.

- Remember that you brain cannot feel emotion in past or future, only the here and now.

Chapter 5

Self-
Actualization

Esteem

Belonging

Safety

Physiological

We now have made it past the four tiers of deficiency needs that must be satisfied in order to reach our potential and be our best self. Although they were important and necessary, now that we have passed the physical, safety, belonging and esteem needs, we can focus on the path to creativity, growth and the ability to help others reach achieve their needs.

- **Feelings Forecast**
- **Emotional Clarity**
- **Talent Quest**
- **Calculated Intention**
- **Interpretive Reflection**

The first section we will discuss how the thought model works and how we can train our thoughts (like other muscles) to improve and be organized. This section outlines a deductive approach to having the best possible relationship with ourselves. Having a good relationship with ourselves and having awareness allows us to have more quality relationships with others. We will also look at the importance and fallouts of being vulnerable. Why it matters to put ourselves in a potential emotional harm's way in order to grow. We will look at the difference between the development of strengths vs. weaknesses, and how to maximize what talents we already have. This chapter will then look at the power and sequence of goal setting, and the importance of setting goals our minds will not reject. This chapter will then wrap up with looking at the importance of embracing our individual efforts to process emotion, be aware of our thoughts and create healthy ways to be hyper-aware of our minds.

Uniquely Exceptional

"Don't let anyone turn your sky into a ceiling"
-Rita Zahara

Feelings Forecast:

As we are on the top of the hierarchy, the first four needs focused on deficiency needs, rather than a being need. Deficiency needs are basically the needs that show up when something is being deprived and you are in a state of survival. Chapter 5 is a high-level depiction of how we can grow and is frankly my favorite part of the hierarchy. Being needs, put emphasis on the achievement of the best versions of ourselves, problem solving and critical thinking.

In this section we are going to look at our thoughts and how simple acts of awareness can lead to healthier relationships with others and ourselves. There is a great model described by Brooke Castillo in her book, "Self-Coaching 101", that states there are five steps to our thought model and it includes: circumstances, thoughts, feelings actions and results (in yet another linear progression). This model is an amazing way to compartmentalize your emotions and to even allow a way to work backwards to restart, if the desired result is not achieved.

When we look at circumstances in our lives, it is reality. It is the world around us based in fact. There are no disputing circumstances, as everyone will agree that human's breathe oxygen or there is gravity. When we look at thoughts, they are our perception of reality. Thoughts are subjective and we do with them as we choose. Feelings are emotions that the brain triggers and reacts to. This is where the internal struggle lives. Depending on what thoughts come in, this is where chemical reactions occur.

We touched briefly on this in Chapter 1 (Stress) and how the release of dopamine can contribute to focus, clarity or increased motivation. Cortisol and epinephrine can be released in this moment, which can cause intolerance, irritability and fear. Endorphins can release relaxed feelings and calmness. Oxytocin can help to create a more empathetic environment. According to JP Phillips, the release of dopamine, endorphins and oxytocin is viewed as the **Angels Cocktail**, which leads to highly favorable behaviors.

Emotions are a physiological feeling that we get from the chemical reactions, that can almost seem tangible. We can produce tears, have digestive issues, have an increased heartrate etc. All of these physiological aspects come from feeling emotions.

The next level is actions, which come after we have experienced the circumstance, thought and feeling. We can have natural responses and learned responses and our actions are responses from the feelings. A natural response could be where fight or flight occurs, as it is a coping method.

Breathing techniques could be a learned response in order to cope with anxiety. Another response could be to love and take care of your children, or committing to a relationship.

Lastly, the result or consequence of our actions leave us at the end of the model. It is the end result and is a natural response to your thoughts. It all depends on how you are thinking. But, within this model things are missing that I would like to bring your attention to.

Myken has spent years as a successful yoga instructor and life coach, and she has determined that there is a need to start with the affect or baseline. We discussed affect in Chapter 4 and it was discussed that in our purest form (babies), they aren't born with opinions. They learn opinions from their support staff and environment.

If we start our model with affect, it can determine how you view your reality or circumstance. Someone who enters a situation in a positive or optimistic mood will view a thunderstorm differently than someone who is in a poor or negative mood. Myken uses yoga, meditation and breathing exercises to calm the parasympathetic nervous system, thus calming the mood to then do thought work. Once she has dissected the useful from the un-useful thoughts, she then uses a guided meditation to help her clients visualize the desired outcome.

Another change that Myken suggests, is to add instinct to the model after circumstance and before thoughts. Malcom Gladwell in his book, "Blink", discussed how important rapid cognition is to our decision making and in that two seconds we make quick judgements and assumptions that come solely from past experiences. This is when the prefrontal cortex could trigger a fight or flight response.

As we look at the hierarchy of needs, we understand the linear path involved to better understand the order of what we must do and it provides kind of a needs by number approach to obtain growth. This next model is the same. It has a hierarchy feel, and all components must be met in order to make it work. With that being said, there is a deductive approach to it, whereas if something is not right in your desired result, you can simply go back to the affected tier and adjust to achieve the desired consequence.

The original model is provided and is followed by the enhanced example of a college student who is having anxiety about completing assignments and how the thought process leads to procrastination and incompletion of tasks.

Thought model:

- Circumstance
- Thought
- Feelings
- Actions
- Result

Student towards the end of a semester:

- Affect- Calm, pleasant and open minded.
- Circumstance- Homework.
- Instinct- Remembering prior experiences about homework being difficult and time consuming.
- Thought- This is overwhelming, and they won't be able to complete the requirement.
- Feelings- Anxiety and frustration.
- Action- turned to binge watch tv and social media.
- Result- Nothing got done.

Then we went back to look at the result and determined that the student wanted the result to reflect homework completion and comprehension. The new model looks like this where we start with the result and work deductively through to the thought.

- Results- Done and understood
- Action- Completed assignments
- Feeling- relief
- Thought- I can get my homework done and I can understand this, even if it is difficult.

In order to be able to change your world you must be willing to take a magnifying glass to and **change your thoughts.** This reset is going to be tough, even with awareness, effort and discipline. It's like a muscle you have to constantly work. If you are willing to rewire the way you think, the outcomes will be so incredibly rewarding and sustainable!

Emotional Clarity:

Emotions are a valuable yet misunderstood part of who we are. This section is designed to understand basic emotions and how they impact us. The first thing I want to cover is that our affect is a baseline of our emotions. Ones affect helps to explain our general mood at any given time and are manifestations of an experienced emotion: expressions, tone, gestures, etc. If you look at a newborn baby, they are unable to communicate with words, so their affect or mood is more than likely unpleasant if they are hungry or need a change of pants.

If we listen to calm music and have candles lit next to us, more than likely our affect is calm. Conversely, loud noises and speeding cars from rush hour lead us to have an alerted affect. **We have lots of natural affects depending on what is going on around us.** This baseline mood can also impact our thinking. If our mood is already agitated, because your kids are rough housing, the phone rings and someone is trying to sell you something that in other situations you would be interested in, our baseline mood is triggered.

This type of understanding is also important for others to better understand us. It is not like we walk down the street telling people how we feel or what is going on in our lives.

Affect can be a useful tool in order to better understand the baselines of others and how we can work with them and also it provides a map for others to break us down as well. If we can have an affect of calmness and serenity, we are far more likely to have productive conversations, critically think and problem solve.

External factors are at play here and can certainly impact your mood. This is why it is so important to create a time to get back to the desired baseline. You know where you want to be, now you have the awareness to get there. Awareness of being in an agitated mood can lead you to find the neutrality that is necessary before making any important decisions. This is where meditation and even yoga are so impactful. Perpetuating a peaceful mood before making important decisions or even lead to creativity.

People think that their emotions control them. I am here telling you that that is not the case. Our emotions have everything to do with how we were raised, our culture that we were raised in and what the people taught us within our inner circle. Emotions are not hardwired, and they are absolutely not universally expressed.

Cultural differences are extremely important to understand when it comes to understanding emotion. If you look at some cultures, women have purposely elongated their necks in order to see how many rings they can wear and that they have no fat or wrinkles. In our culture, women have fat sucked out of places just so they can inject it into other places. Our culture also finds augmentation of body parts beautiful. Cultures decide for themselves what is beautiful and sometimes the definition is universal, however sometimes it is not. Beauty can lead to status and status can lead to beauty; they are seemingly interchangeable.

We are raised to think that within culture there is beauty and the same goes for emotions. People raised in different cultures can curate different responses to external stimuli. In some Asian cultures, the men are taught to look stern, not to smile and have perpetual poker faces (hence no affect). These same cultures don't handshake or touch to show respect, however they bow from a distance. We may have a hard time reading people from different cultures due to the emotions not being universally expressed and being brought on by different external factors.

Emotions are not hardwired in the brain; we were taught how to be afraid of different things. Out here in the Southwest, I was taught to be afraid of snakes and scorpions. I am assuming that people from Alaska have never experienced a scorpion, so their brain has no idea how to process it, unless they've been educated about them.

Emotions are nothing but the brains best guess at how to handle a specific situation. What your brain constructs at the moment of emotion is completely based on past experiences. All thoughts about things come from previous experience and beliefs about the external world and yourself.

If your brain has never seen something before, it will try to figure out what it is and it is not always right. Sometimes the formula is broken and the guess is wrong. It could be a new behavior that you haven't seen or experienced yet or a new quarrel in your relationships. Our brains will construct thoughts around it based on what has happened and more importantly, what has been proven successful in the past.

When situations come up that are similar to past experiences, our affect becomes alerted. For example, if we had an abusive stepmom who was cruel and manipulative while we were growing up, then we are presented with an individual at work who displays similar behaviors. We may then have a fight or flight response, as our brain knows we have been down this road before, and thinks we are going down it again. It is like we are all walking around with varying degrees of our own personal PTSD, and we each have triggers.

Before we further discuss triggers and emotions, I want to discuss some things that could come before triggers and if the awareness of these are realized, and metacognition is utilized, the triggers may not be as impactful, however I fully understand that they are real and need attention.

When we look at micro triggers or pet peeves, I think about things that could potentially lead to triggers. Pet peeves, can be things that provide a slow burn in a relationship or with total strangers. If you were to look back at the Stress section of this book, we discussed how buffering can lead to addiction if not careful and without awareness. In this scenario, I feel that pet peeves can be thwarted off and not made triggers, as long as awareness is realized, which can be extremely beneficial when we are looking to uncover healing and coping mechanisms. Also, below is additional information on triggers and emotions.

Some examples of Pet Peeves:
- People speaking over someone
- Eating with mouth open
- Not holding the door open for someone
- Not cleaning up after one's self
- Condescension

Information regarding Triggers:

- From the past
- Needs safety to process
- Personalized
- Can be a surprise from the subconscious
- Can result in physiological symptoms

Emotions

- Based in conscious thought
- Experiential
- Not hardwired
- Best guess from prior experience
- Needs safety to process

Talent Quest:

I wanted to add this section because what is being missed in our culture is people who are truly exceptional at things. Not only are we looking to further develop our talents and strengths, we are also looking to fully understand what they are.

Every semester I ask my students if they had the choice to either develop their strengths or weaknesses; they mostly say that they would rather become more well-rounded and work on developing their weaknesses.

To my surprise and disbelief, I start asking questions to this group and begin to uncover why they would prefer to go this route. Many say that they would be able to help more people if they know a little about a lot. Others say they don't want to have too much of a focus on any one thing, as they may miss out on future opportunities.

Contrary to the belief of my past classes, I am of the opinion that we are all blessed with specific talents and the earlier we can identify and further develop these talents, the better we will become. Talent development is a concern that I see with the youth today. We have kids who are content with their abilities and more or less take them for granted (sort of looks like a "fixed" mindset).

I always communicate to my students that I would always choose to develop my talents, as that is what makes me unique and I have a strong need to be exceptional at things vs. being average. I have even taken the stance that not only shouldn't people try to develop their weaknesses, they should stay the hell away from them!

For quite some time I have told people that I: talk way to fast, I have a difficult time letting things go, I don't forgive as easily as I should, and I have atrocious handwriting. But guess what? I have no desire to change any of these things because I spend 99% of my time working on the development of my strengths and talents. I focus on things that help me stand out in a crowd and things that will add value to my life (as we previously discussed). Being exceptional at things will help you build confidence and connect with others with similar skillsets.

When I look at strengths, I want to make sure that they are things that can be developed. Understandably, we all can't play shortstop for the Diamondbacks, but we can all take a good hard look at what we already do well, and how we can make it better.

There is a great website that helps you to take a test and understand your strengths for free. The website is, "**high5test.com**", and it provides a great baseline to understand what you are already good at. My results focused on things like: self-confident, lover of learning and developing others potential. These things I believe are tangible and I can formulate a plan to maximize my abilities and growth in these areas. For example, there are categories like, believer, thinker, winner, or philomath (plus many more). Ultimately, pointing you in the direction of development.

Everyone is a genius, but if you judge a fish by its ability to climb a tree, it will live its whole life believing it is stupid.

-Albert Einstein

When looking at the quote above, we need to make an honest effort to understand how our authentic selves relate to our strengths. If we are a monkey in a tree climbing competition, great. If we are a goldfish in the same situation, we need to look for the pool, and not settle for the fact that we can't climb a tree. There are differences between what you are good at vs what you are passionate about. The goal here is to try to find a balance between the two. Typically, one follows the other, but not always, and it is not always linear. The top tier of any profession can lead to a very solid life, a solid living, and have the fruits that this world can offer. **Master your craft!**

The cool thing about strengths, and this could just be my perception, is that typically you enjoy things you are good at. So, when I take the time to read books on leadership or how to be a better coach, I actually enjoy it, which makes it all that much easier.

Now just because it's easier, doesn't mean it's easy. To go back to creating positive habits, if you would like to formulate a plan of attack in order to develop your strengths, be aware that it may take some time, patience and discipline. When we factor in all the components of creating positive habits, we have already discussed all the aspects (except one, which is next).

Another thing to consider when understanding your talents, is to be mindful of the fact that your talents are not static. For the most part they will be similar for the long term, however, be aware that over the course of time, our lives and personalities may/probably will change.

Keep in mind that strengths are not all hard or soft skills. Strengths are all encompassing, as your strength could be that fact that you are disciplined enough to be motivated. You may have events in your life that make you more or less empathetic. You may have opportunities that allow you to develop more or less leadership skills.

Just because your strengths are where they are, doesn't mean they won't morph into something else. This may seem a bit like becoming more well-rounded and working on your weaknesses, but I can assure you that this is just the evolution of strengths throughout the course of your life.

It isn't normal to know what we want. It is a rare and difficult psychological achievement.

-Abraham Maslow

Calculated Intention:

This section dives into how we should be creating our goals and how to ensure follow-through in order to maximize success as well as confidence in the goal making process. Think about what is keeping you from your goals. Is it the ability to articulate them, dream them, believe in yourself or feel silly trying something new? We all must have our needs met in order to feel worthy of aspirations, have confidence in ourselves and not be in survival mode.

When in survival mode our goals are basic and short term. Things like food, shelter and water are top priorities. When our needs are met, we are able to accomplish great things and really push towards amplified capabilities. When I have something in mind that I would like to accomplish, I put it into one of four categories to help organize how I can best ensure completion.

Don't be fearful when looking at your dreams,
Despite of how contentment currently seems.

The first category I use is **short term goals**. Now this may seem a bit redundant as there have been many writings on this topic, which is why we won't spend a ton of time here. Short term goals are goals that I see myself completing in the next ninety days. These have been identified as goals that I can easily see and the path to achievement has been identified.

The next level of goals is **intermediate.** With intermediate goals, the focus is on the next three to six months. The intermediate goals are a little farther off and should still be relatively attainable, in terms of ability to complete.

Thirdly we have **long terms goals** which is anything that you expect to complete after six months. This could be an important goal that moderates urgency. It could be a somewhat lofty goal, but still it has a relatively high likelihood of being completed.

Now we get to my favorite goal which was described by Chris McChesney in his book, "The Four Disciplines of Execution", whereas a **wildly important goal (WIG)** is crucial to keep your eyes down field and understand that even though a goal may be lofty, that doesn't mean you shouldn't strive for it.

A way that I try to bring the wildly important goal into the mix and make it pragmatic, is that I look to implement a daily activity goal sheet in order to keep track of where I stand in regard to any goal I have. A few pages from here, is an example of a daily activity sheet that I would use in order to keep track of the process of how I was performing in order to achieve my short-term goals.

I have found that the pursuit of short terms goals, accompanied by a process in place, allows you to see in real time how your effort is contributing to your success. The example I am going to use is for an overall goal, then the sub goals are included in order for me to organize how I will get there.

My daily active goals are not static, and can change as often as I would like them too. In fact, they need to change as the goals are starting to be completed in order to achieve the new ones that are constantly being formed. Keep in mind that it acts a bit like a carousel, as once goals are achieved, new ones are constantly being added to keep the cycle going.

-For example - Overall goal is to be in better shape, to look and feel better while returning to compete in athletic competitions.

- Short term goal- lose weight and be healthier, start a fasting program and light weight training.
- Intermediate goal-loss of around twenty-thirty pounds in three months with my fasting program,

adding distance to my runs whilst lowering times and starting to enter low impact competitions.

- Long term goal- continue to increase my weight loss in a healthy manner and increase my stamina and athletic ability.

- Wildly important goal-I would like to enter an Ultra-Marathon in Maricopa County in February of 2022 that consists of a sixty-mile run.

Here is the beginning of my daily activity tracker so I know exactly where I am on a given day. I add the goal and the date, followed by whether or not it was executed and during the description I have a measure of 1-5 on how I felt about the activity and lastly, I add highlights.

Health goal 11/30/20	Done	Description
Ran 6 miles	x	5- 57:45
Fasted- noon and 6am	x	4- ended at 11:45
Current Weight	x	4-199 lbs. (3 down)
Prepped food for a.m.	x	4- burger, pickle
Arms at the gym	x	3- 4 sets out of 7

I find that the daily tracker sets the tone for the entire goal making process. If you want to build in a cheat day or an off day, that is absolutely no problem, just document it so that you are aware of all the data. Problems persist when there are gaps and you don't feel the need to continue to update the table. This sheet needs to be built in as a changed behavior.

I have a special notebook that I handwrite this information in, that is free of distraction and allows me to focus on the task at hand. I feel that there is more of a connection and better intentions when I handwrite something down. It incorporates different learning modalities (kinesthetic, auditory and visual) and works really well for me. Taking a deductive approach really helps as I am then able to see the end goal and work backwards identifying each individual step that needs to be completed along the way.

The goal cycle needs to perpetuate by eventually moving the wildly important goal to long term, the long-term goal to intermediate and intermediate to short term. That is the way to see change as your goals are dynamic. Be aware of the changes your goals may go through. The main point of this section is to be aware of the process and to make it your own. Your daily activity sheet can contain anything you want, just keep it consistent and weed it frequently. **When we constantly cycle the goals**

through from WIG to short term, we are creating a habit of focusing on the process vs. focusing on the destination. An example of this is dedicating time to physical fitness in order to be an athlete, instead of just wanting to compete in a marathon. At some point the marathon date will come and go, whereas being an athlete has permanence.

Another key concept in dealing with goals is temptation. This word is generally looked upon as a religious term as something that is evil taking us away from something good. Really, temptation is any thoughts that are preventing you from having the life you want. For example, if you want to have a strong marriage, then temptation would be any thoughts taking your whole self away from your spouse. The awareness of value-added relationships, panning out the gravel as well as safeguarding your worth will certainly help with this.

The sky is the limit with your goals! Get out there and do something remarkable. I know you have it in you and I know that the desire is there. Just look at a way to carve out the time and set small goals as a path to achievement. Go learn that language or instrument, travel, open a new business. Stop being bogged down and overwhelmed with thoughts suffocating your potential and find a way to make it happen!

If needed, reach out to a coach to help with accountability and performance. This can help you from being overwhelmed and stagnant in your pursuit of growth.

Initially, it is not your ability that matters, it is your availability!

Interpretative Reflection:

Now that we have a better understanding of how emotions work, now we can discuss how they impact self-actualization. **Self-actualization is a path that you create in your mind. It comes from the willingness to experience negative emotion. If you are willing to experience defeat, judgement and humiliation, you will increase your levels of growth.**

What if you didn't worry about judgement or failure, would you go after things 100%? If you are not afraid of negative emotion then you would be willing to try anything? **The worst part about mistakes are what you make them mean.** The secret to self-confidence is to not beat yourself up. We will discuss this in greater detail later in this chapter, however you need to be your own advocate, be committed to your passion and have your own back! Don't be afraid to try things, the worst that can happen is whatever you want it to be.

When we discuss **Metacognition** or one's ability to observe their own thought process, there are a few misconceptions that I like to provide additional information about, which are crucial to understanding how we process negative emotions. It is kind of like having the initial

223

discussion with toddlers and asking them to slow down and use their words. They know what they want, the harder thing is to be aware of the thoughts behind it and communicate accordingly.

First, **you are not your problems.** We often think about: social status, our careers, even our appearance, as who we are. Some people view these things as more important than they are, as they even experience a high when things are going well. The flip side of this, is that they are devastated when they go away. These things are not who we are. You are worthy with or without those things. Myken is constantly seeing this with her female life coaching clients, as they struggle with aging.

The second important thing is that **you are not your brain**. What is going on in your brain is not who you are. We know this because you are able to observe your brain think. What part of you is thinking about your thinking? You must separate what you are thinking, so you can intentionally decide what to think on purpose. The ability to step back and view what is going on internally, allows you to disconnect from your biological psychology.

The third crucial factor when dealing with negative emotions is that **you don't need to wait for the world to change in order to be happy**. Your reality will be exactly what it is, and there is obviously no way to change it. **The key here is that you don't have to wait for circumstances around you to change before you can feel the way that you want.** Feeling is good, it brings awareness to the physiological side of emotion. It is a great centering mechanism that allows us to be aware of how external factors affects our homeostasis.

The fourth key point I wanted to make deals more with life's natural counterweight. We have to be able to **take the good with the bad,** otherwise we wouldn't know what the good is. Life is about experiencing all things put in our path, don't forget that not making choices due to being overwhelmed, still leads to making choices. The choice is not making a choice, and as we all know, **choices have consequences (consequences are not always negative).** We control more than we think and our action needs to lead toward our own personal finish line or at least checkpoints along the way.

Finally, the last point I wanted to bring to your attention is that **you are able to assimilate your results**. Plain and simple. Whether or not you make a conscious effort for something or it happens by default, you will end up being who you choose to be. This is why awareness is paramount as you point out which way you are going.

225

We are beginning to scratch the surface on this topic and we will go into much more actionable detail in the next chapter. I really just want you to begin thinking about how much control you actually have in your life and how to make sure you can be fulfilled and be who you want. In Chapter 5, I will provide a model to break down individual situations and take a look at how to create your desired reality.

There are a few more concepts that I feel are important when we talk about negative emotion and how they factor into our self-confidence. I look at the world we live in and everyone is busy with constantly apologizing. Men and women alike have gotten in the habit of taking the word, "sorry" and using it as a buffer for any uncomfortable situations. We say sorry when we feel like others need to hear it, we say sorry when we don't know what else to do, and honestly it feels like the times we should say it, we don't. **All saying you're sorry means is that you care more about the relationship with the other person, than you do your own pride.**

So how do we move away from actions that aren't genuine and authentic and prepare ourselves to deal with tough situations?

There are specific things that we should focus on that I view as **dirty discomfort**.

- Vulnerability from insecurity
- Not willing to be embarrassed
- Not willing to fail
- Not willing to be rejected
- Not willing to be your authentic self

These excerpts do nothing but hold us back. We talked in Chapter 1 about how cravings can suffocate what you really want to do. In Chapter 5, we will discuss more about mindsets, but here and now, the inability to be vulnerable and uncomfortable will squash out all ability and focus to take the next step to awesomeness.

Here are a few examples of **clean discomfort** that put us in the driver's seat, despite how scared or nervous they make us.

- Vulnerability from confidence
- Willing to face adversity
- Wiliness to try new things
- Willing to upset others
- Willing to be your authentic self!

We must be willing to put ourselves in these positions to grow and build our esteem. It is going to be tough in the beginning, it is going to be nerve racking and uncomfortable. That's fine, one of my favorite sayings is, **"there is no growth in the comfort zone and no comfort in the growth zone"**. Just think back to when I mentioned how tough it was the first time I grew a mustache. It was weird and I felt strange in public, but after multiple attempts of mustachery, it literally grew on me and I had a different perspective with multiple exposures. Now I mustache you a question, do you allow self-esteem development to be the driving force behind your explorations? :)

I also often think about couples who have been married for a while and one/both of them go through a mid-life crisis. We all may have our own stereotype of what this could look like, with younger romantic partners, being more social or purchasing an extravagant car. The question I posit, **"Is a mid-life crisis more about freaking out about where you are in life and proceeding to do drastic things, or is it just a way to finally return to being your most authentic self?"**

Something else to think about with this is that, if a mid-life crisis is inevitable and we all go through

something like this, then why can't we reframe it to ask, why can't the 'now' game be the 'end' game?

What is holding us back from being authentic now, or possibly before a mid-life crisis? Are we too involved in our careers to make the money we think we need to try and impress people we don't like?

A mid-life crisis does not reveal that men like women or that women like men, it also does not reveal that men like fast cars and motorcycles. You heard it here first folks, men have always liked fast cars and even faster women. This authentic reveal typically takes place when adults are in a place of their needs being met. No more worries of health care or getting their kids set up for success. Once we are in this place, the mid-life authenticity transformation begins!

The last point I want to make in this section discussing metacognition is how defense mechanisms are utilized in our lives. All metacognition is, is a heightened awareness of how we process our emotions. Here are some examples of defense mechanisms as depicted by Reeve in his book, "Understanding Motivation and Emotion". It is up to you to better understand your processing and how to benefit from said awareness. **Keep in mind that defense mechanisms are simply a way for us to have more control over our emotions!**

Anticipation- Where we are worried about future danger, so we manufacture small steps in order to cope. *Bobby got a great job and is concerned about it being too good, so he plots out the steps of how it will come to an end.*

Denial- Blatant ignoring of undesired circumstances. *There is no way that I didn't get invited to the party, this must be some mistake. Did they mistype my email?*

Projection- Pushing your own issues or behaviors onto someone else. *I am miserable in my inability to lose weight, so instead I blast others for being overweight.*

Regression- Pushing back to an earlier time or behavior. *When my Grandfather passed, he took me to the top of a mountain, that I will be visiting shortly in order to replicate feelings.*

Humor- Not taking yourself too seriously, deflecting un-comfortability by accepting shortcomings. *During uncomfortable times, I make fun of my hair or shirt, as the un-comfortability of this situation is too much for me to handle.*

Displacement- Delivering an emotion to someone or something other than you. *Molly had a difficult day at work and was invalidated multiple times. At her favorite Mexican restaurant that night, she was rude and vile to her server, who seemingly kept messing up her order.*

Fantasy- Displaying gratifying achievements and desires in place of reality. *Our social media lives. Some may not like who they are in real life, so they put unnatural levels of energy and time into creating/maintaining their existence in cyberspace.*

Rationalization- Justifying suspect behaviors, by providing a logical reason to feel a given way. *Brian was justifying how controlling he is in his current relationship, by stating how his past girlfriend had been unfaithful.*

Reaction Formation- Actively displaying cognitive dissonance and doing the opposite of a true motive or feeling. *Young boys typically bully young girls who they are attracted too. Alluding to unconventional ways of showing interest.*

Sublimation- Drawing energy from a challenging emotional process into another more socially acceptable one. *Peggy just got out of a long relationship and has decided instead of dealing with her emotions, she has determined that a better use of her time is to dive into Pinterest and re-organize her entire home.*

Identification- Transferring personal characteristics onto someone more successful/powerful/popular. *Kesha was new in school and thought the best way to fit in, was to begin to dress/act like the popular students.*

One more concept of metacognition is to understand our own **Time Horizons** as it pertains to goals and needs. These time horizons span out farther and farther due to how regulated our needs are and act as a barometer to know why it's hard for people to get out of a bad situation, leave a dangerous neighborhood or worry about their professional/personal futures.

If you think about a homeless person who is worried about simply finding clean water or their next meal. Their time horizon is typically about 24 hours. Someone who is living in fear, may have a view of about 48 hours. Someone who is struggling with or just started a relationship, they probably strive to the how's and what's, that will appear as they grow as their time horizon spans out with that individual, and possibly the duration of time to raise a family (15-20 years). If you look at someone with high self-esteem, they are more than likely focused on the stock market, and how retirement will affect them. Their horizon spans through their lift time. Lastly, if you look at someone who is actualized, they are probably concerned with climate change and world peace, as their time horizon probably spans past their own lifetime. More in terms of their legacy. Try to look at your own personal goals to see which time horizon you fall under and to detect which needs level you are deficient in.

Being hyper-aware of these things adds to our owner's manual and will only help with understanding our emotional fortitude and will provide sustainable relationships. The ability to understand our own individual thoughts from a scientific standpoint is an interesting concept as well. Ryan Bush coined the term **Psychitecture** in his Book, "Designing the Mind", to better understand our own psychological evolution and to improve our operating system.

Regulation of our nervous systems are extremely important. **Dysregulated nervous systems** can lead to erratic thinking, behaviors and breathing. We may feel physically numb, clumsy, forgetful and scatterbrained. Regulating your nervous system can look like: being in touch with feelings, understanding needs, and communicating said needs/feelings. **Another huge component here is that when your heart rate goes above 150 beats per minute, your ability to critically think and problem solve goes down (and the rate continues every 10 beats per minute).** *This is why it may seem like time is flying by when in a tough workout. You are strictly surviving vs. worrying about how much time is left.*

Summary:

- Feelings Forecast allows a deductive approach to changing our thoughts.
- If you can change your thoughts you can change your life.
- Separate your emotions from circumstance, stop controlling others, manipulating and blaming.
- Pay attention to the hierarchy of thoughts and work deductively to make your path.
- Affects are moods or baselines.
- Emotions are guesses and are triggered by circumstances and thought.
- Awareness of pet peeves can uncover healing and coping mechanisms.
- Triggers vs Emotions
- We are taught to process emotions through our culture.
- We can regulate our affect.
- Identify and focus on the development of your talents.

- Identify and keep distance from your weaknesses.
- Take time to periodically understand your strengths as they are not static.
- Develop what makes you unique and exceptional.
- Be aware of and stay away from temptations in your lives, as this could be one of the main reasons for lack of goal attainment.
- Effort and discipline are key motivators when looking to develop.
- Take time to reflect upon your short term, intermediate, long term and wildly important goals.
- Create and maintain a daily active tracker that you can realistically maintain and update often.
- With upkeep you will be able to cycle your goals. Your wild goal will become your long term, long term to intermediate and intermediate to short term.
- The daily active tracker allows you to focus on the process and your individual effort.

- Metacognition is one's own ability to observe their own thought processes.
- You are not your problems or your brain.
- Don't wait to be happy, life is feeling all the things.
- Mid-life crisis- A way to return to our most authentic selves?
- Coping and defense mechanisms are normal and awareness is crucial.
- Constantly update your owner's manual or your operating systems.
- Regulate your nervous system
- Be aware of how time horizons affect your goals.
- Keep heart rate low or immerse into survival state.

Positive Change Spark

*"There's a Darkness Upon Me, that's Flooded
in Light"*
Head Full of Doubt/Road Full of Promise-
The Avett Brothers

Striving to be a positive change spark, whilst utilizing the hierarchy of needs, is the overwhelming message within this book. The prior chapters have provided some strategies and concepts to try and put together tools and best practices in order to not only identify paths to change, but to show you how to walk down them and help others to obtain.

This section provides a breakdown of the greatest hits of this book and shows a simplified and boiled down approach to growth (shown below):

1. **Move**
2. **Value**
3. **Help**
4. **Worth**
5. **Authenticity**

When I say, **"move"**, what I am intending to be capitalized on, is to not be sedentary or static. Obviously, there are physical affects that exercise has on your body, but I am more interested on the mental consequences of being active and dynamic. Exercise magnifies the consanguinity between biology and psychology. This relationship helps to release endorphins and dopamine that helps with creativity, problem solving, focus, motivation and critical thinking. I like to use exercise as a form of active meditation that forces the ability to simple-task and utilize the sub-conscious in ways that I was previously unable to during the normal drudgery of my day. **Keep in mind that sweating and crying, allows a valve of release to let go of thought pressure.**

Through the sweat comes connection!

The "**value**" portion of this section looks to show the importance of value-added relationships and activities, and looks to streamline our lives to maximize value added scenarios. This includes spending time with people that matter and limiting the noise in our lives. Remember we discussed cutting out all the aspects of our lives that don't make us better. Thinking to ourselves, does this help me or hurt me? Or even less drastic, does this help me or not? We discussed the value in modulating the information we consume and it was almost like we were panning for gold, only the gold was value. The key takeaway here is to always be on the lookout for value and to create/maintain behaviors that support that view. Strive for and protect your most valuable, yet non-renewable resource- **TIME!**

Don't sacrifice the real,
In search of the ideal

"**Help**", I feel is moderately self-explanatory, the kicker is to use this verb more regularly. Help as many people and as often as you can. Utilize extreme feats of kindness and allow yourself to understand the reciprocity of service. Helping others feels amazing and the more we can manufacture opportunities to help others, the more often we will seek out the feeling of the goodness in doing so. Helping others includes helping yourself! Another aspect of this is to keep top of mind the things you are thankful for and archive the actions and feelings associated. Then come back to that list as often as possible. Actively create and seek out reminders of how helping others has affected you. It also entails the freedom from fear in asking for help/being vulnerable, as you want to give others the opportunity to experience the benefits of aid.

The quickest way to mental health,
is to be available to someone else!

"**Worth**", means to understand your worth and to keep records of past successes no matter the size. You are worthy of praise, gratitude and love. There is value in failing, being vulnerable and being resilient to persevere with success and happiness. Look to change the ingredients in your brain and be aware of how to make internal changes in order to help relationships with others as well as yourself. You are worthy of love as you are human!

Shy away from doubting your Worth, Simply because you were put here on Earth

Lastly, **"authenticity"** focus' on being your real self. Work on being real in all relationships, not just romantic. Work on having difficult conversations, partnership equivalence and that your expectations align with outcomes. You don't need to be sadistic or narcissistic to be real with people. **If you are not authentic, all you are doing is wasting time.** It is never too late to be the real you! Don't put it off any longer, and maintain this at all costs. I often view authenticity as a "**Rubik's Cube Racket**", (popular '80s toy) whereas I look at some specific aspect of my life, let's just say teaching for this example. I try to teach a way that all the blue squares will like. In doing so, all the other colors are upset and don't get what they want. If I try to then teach in a way that the orange squares will like, then the blue are upset and the other colors are disorganized. Ultimately, be yourself and you will at minimum, remain consistent and expectations will be realized.

There is no intimacy,
Without Authenticity

In conclusion, there will be times that you are going to be flat out exhausted from the journey, tired from trying! Use this time to understand how you feel and that it is more important to reformulate and **focus on the process**, as there has got to be something more to do. Don't give up, just keep learning, experimenting and create habits of perseverance and resilience. There is tremendous power when we examine attitude and effort. These are the key drivers to success.

We discussed earlier that it is so important to not lie to ourselves, as you cannot manufacture feelings. In looking to beat a dead horse, we must make the choice to change our behaviors over time as nothing is immediate and without challenges. If you manufacture an important emotion or feeling, your mind will automatically reject it and you will be in the same place you started.

The overwhelming goal is to be better today than you were yesterday and that message is completely subjective. If you are striving for growth and your mind knows you are authentic, then there is no stopping you. Keep the correlation positive between changed behaviors and your growth. If you can do that, then you have wrangled your inner conflict and all that lies ahead are gains.

There is another Buddhist saying to develop a strong backside and to have a soft belly. I feel like many of us have the exact opposite. We shield out love and authenticity, while being very susceptible and sensitive to things we cannot control, from people we barely know and for reasons we probably cannot explain. Look to develop your backside and be more open with your heart! According to John Kim, The Angry Therapist, **never sacrifice your truth for membership!**

In this life we are constantly looking for the right path or to make the right decisions. It is vital to make sure we look at the right circumstances to provide clarity to our lives. We discussed "Addiction", back in Chapter 1 and discussed how the addiction was actually to feel consciousness and not the multitude of things that one can be addicted too. Consciousness or being present is at the forefront of clarity as well. After sex, drinking coffee/alcohol going for a trail run, allows for a different perspective on how to make decisions and/or problem solve. Being present does not

244

allow for fear of the future or guilt from the past, as being present allows for true authentic choice.

When you have difficultly in front of you, don't be afraid to go out in nature, work up a sweat, be grateful for your blessings and surroundings in order to better be in the moment, as that is where the solutions will be found. **Jordan Peterson said that you must transform yourself into a monster in order to stay safe, then proceed with discipline and harness it, in order to be your best and stay alive!**

One of my favorite sayings is, "I am a traveler, not a mapmaker". I have previously viewed analogous maps as I would in old '80s video games, where the map showed you where you were vs. where you need to go. Now is the time to make your own map **AND** be the traveler. Hopefully with discussing needs concepts in this book, I have helped show you where you are, but it is up to you to build a map that uncovers where you want to go, and how to get there.

Just know the Kingdom of God is within you,
Even though the battle is bound to continue
-True Sadness, The Avett Brothers

Example of my daily routine in the pursuit of joy and fulfillment!

First day of the rest of my life	Quote- There is no intimacy without authenticity	X
Gratitude	I am thankful for my wife, my job(s) and my children's health	X-5
Exercise	6 mile jog/hike/run, Skyline Regional Park	X-5+
Meditation	30 minutes of breath focus and active introspection (intention is key)	X-5
Extreme Feats of Kindness	Text 2 people I care about, and tell them how/why I care about them.	X-5+ told 3 peeps
Journaling about recent success	Talk about another successful semester teaching at	X-5
Consumption	Fasted from Noon to 6am Desire for healthier intake	X-4 Doritos and candy

Summary:

- Look for opportunities to be a positive change spark in all aspects of your life.
- Move- Exercise more in order to reap, physical and mental health benefits.
- Value- Look for as many value added situations in your life in order to maintain them and create more.
- Help- Devote unrenewable resources to as many people and as often as you can, in the end it will end up helping you.
- Worth- you are worthy of love, happiness and compassion.
- Authenticity- Be your real self despite it being challenging in the beginning.
- Set yourself up for Clarity.
- Be better today than you were yesterday.
- Don't waste your most valuable asset-Time.
- Be your own mapmaker!

Recommended listening for Different levels of growth opportunities.
No particular order and with no descriptions or understanding of how they make me feel.
No leading the witness here and no manufacturing your top of mind.

- ✓ November Blue- The Avett Brothers
- Fix You- Coldplay
- Falls on Me- Fuel
- Until I Fall Away- Gin Blossoms
- Angels of the Silences- Counting Crows
- Don't Look Back in Anger- Oasis
- Where is My Mind- The Pixies
- ✓ From Now On- Zach Brown Band
- Hero- Family of the Year
- Black Balloon- Goo Goo Dolls
- Romeo and Juliet- The Killers
- Into the Mystic- The Wallflowers
- Charmed- My Friend Steve
- Sick Cycle Carousel- Lifehouse
- ✓ Slide Away- Oasis
- Read My Mind- The Killers
- Cleopatra- The Lumineers
- Spirits- The Strumbellas
- Run- Snow Patrol
- Let Down- Radiohead
- The Funeral- Band of Horses
- ✓ Clouds- BORNS
- Fade into You- Mazzy Star
- Man of the Hour- Pearl Jam
- If it's the Beaches- The Avett Brothers
- ✓ Riser- Dirks Bentley
- Hurt- Johnny Cash

- Off he Goes- Pearl Jam
- Shimmer- Shawn Mullins
- Fly from Heaven- Toad the Wet Sprocket
- Lucky Man- The Verve
- Don't Follow- Alice in Chains
- I am the Highway- Audioslave
- Morning Song- The Avett Brothers
- The Story- Brandi Carlyle
- Sedona-Houndmouth
- Hallelujah- Jeff Buckley
- The Man- The Killers
- Stubborn Love- The Lumineers
- Forever (Garage Version)- Mumford & Sons
- Starlight- Muse
- Dream Catch Me- Newton Faulkner
- Sirens- Pearl Jam
- Chasing the Daylight- Phillip LaRue
- Black Star-Radiohead
- The Scientist- Coldplay
- Hands Down-Dashboard Confessional
- Not Only Numb- Gin Blossoms
- Bird Set Free- Sia
- Patience- Chris Cornell
- How Far we've Come- Matchbox Twenty
- Comes and Goes in Waves- Greg Laswell
- Where'd You Go- Fort Minor
- Motorcycle Drive By- Third Eye Blind

252

- The Humpty Dumpty Love Song-Travis
- Wounded- Third Eye Blind
- Beautiful Wreck- Shawn Mullins
- Fire Escape- Fastball
- The First Single- The Format
- I Wish I Was- The Avett Brothers
- All I Need- Radiohead
- Smile- Pearl Jam
- Free as a Bird- The Beatles
- Street Spirit (Fade Out)- Radiohead
- Nobody Knows- The Lumineers
- Lovers in Japan/Reign of Love- Coldplay
- Murder in the City- The Avett Brothers
- Beloved One (Live)- Ben Harper
- Singing in my Sleep- Semisonic
- Kansas City- The New Basement Tapes
- Guaranteed- Eddie Vedder
- Donna- The Lumineers
- Rocket- The Smashing Pumpkins
- Say Yes- Elliott Smith
- Nothing Else Matters- Godsmack
- Society- Eddie Vedder
- No Hard Feelings- The Avett Brothers
- Bright Lights- Matchbox Twenty
- Mekong- The Refreshments
- The Drugs don't Work- The Verve
- If I Ever Leave this World Alive-Flogging Molly

- Sleep on the Floor- The Lumineers
- When my Time Comes- Dawes
- Angel's Wings (acoustic)- Social Distortion
- Rise- Eddie Vedder
- God of Wine- Third Eye Blind
- Maybe it's Time- Bradley Cooper
- High Steppin'- The Avett Brothers
- Just Breathe- Pearl Jam
- Slow it Down (Live)- The Lumineers
- Pork and Beans- Weezer
- All these things that I've done- The Killers
- Give it Up- The Format
- Karma Police- Radiohead
- Blood- The Middle East
- True Sadness- The Avett Brothers
- A.M. Radio- The Lumineers
- Another Story- The Head and the Heart
- Heat Above- Greta Van Fleet
- Anyway (mellow piano version)- Dynamite Hack
- Come Back- Pearl Jam

Notes and Recommended Reading/Viewing:

Achor, S. (2010). The Happiness Advantage: The seven principles of positive psychology that fuel success and performance at work (1st Ed.). New York, NY: Broadway Books.

Achor, S. (2013). Before Happiness: The 5 hidden keys to achieving success, spreading happiness, and sustaining positive change.

Achor, S. (2018). Big Potential (1st Ed.). New York, NY: Currency.

Amadio, D. (2020). Ted Talk: The Flip Phone Manifesto. https://www.youtube.com/watch?v=SjzxsTG6OaE

Brown, B. (2018). Dare to Lead: Brave work, tough conversations, whole hearts. New York: Random House LLC.

Brown, B. (2012). Daring Greatly: How the courage to be vulnerable transforms the way we live, love, parent, and lead. New York, NY: Gotham Books

Brown, H. (1973). The Currant Bush. https://www.churchofjesuschrist.org/study/new-era/1973/01/the-currant-bush?lang=eng

Bush, R. (2021). Designing the Mind: The Principles of Psychitecture. 2021

Castillo, B. (2009). Self-Coaching 101:Use your Mind, don't let it use you.

Cherry, K. (2020). Harry Harlow and the Nature of Affection. https://www.verywellmind.com/harry-harlow-and-the-nature-of-love-2795255

Cohen, S. (2015). The Day Women Went on Strike. Time Magazine, August 26, 2015. https://time.com/4008060/women-strike-equality-1970/

Duckworth, A. (2016). GRIT: The Power of Passion and Perseverance. Scribner

Dweck, C. S. (2006). Mindset: The new psychology of success (1st Ed.). New York, NY: Random House.

Eagleman, D. (2020). Livewired: The inside story of the ever-changing brain. Pantheon Books, New York.

Edmondson, A. (2018). The Fearless Organization: Creating Psychological Safety in the Workplace for Learning, Innovation, and Growth. John Wiley and Sons, Inc.

Galloway, S. (2019). The Algebra of Happiness: Notes on the Pursuit of Success, Love, and Meaning. Penguin Random House

Gladwell, M. (2005). Blink: The Power of Thinking without Thinking. Little, Brown and Company, Time Warner Book Group.

Grant, A. (2013). Give and take: A revolutionary approach to success. Hachette UK.

Luthans, F., Youssef, C., & Avolio, B. (2007). Psychological capital: Developing the competitive human edge. Oxford University Press.

Kaufman, J. (2014). How to Learn Anything Fast: The First 20 Hours. Portfolio

Kim, J. (2019). I Used to be a Miserable F*ck. An Everyman's Guide to a Meaningful Life. HarperOne

Knight, S. (2015). The Life-Changing Magic of Not Giving a F*ck: how to stop spending time you don't have with people you don't like doing things you don't want to do. Little, Brown and Company

Krumwiede, A. (2014). Attachment Theory According to John Bowlby and Mary Ainsworth. GRIN Verlag

Olien, D. (2015). SuperLife: The 5 Simple Fixes that will make Healthy, Fit and Eternally Awesome. HarperCollins Publishers.

Maslow, A. (1943). A Theory of Human Motivation. Psychological Review 50.4. (1943): 370.

Milburn, J., Nicodemus, R. (2016). The Art of Letting Go: The Minimalists. TedxFargo https://www.youtube.com/watch?v=w7rewjFNiys

Penn, S. (2007). Into the Wild

Phillips, D. (2017). Magical Science of Storytelling. https://www.youtube.com/watch?v=Nj-hdQMa3uA

Reeve, J. (2009). Understanding Motivation and Emotion. USA, Wiley.

Roosevelt, T. (1910). The Man in the Arena. Citizenship in a Republic. Speech, April 23, 1910.

Samuelson, R. (2010). The Great Inflation and its Aftermath: The Past and Future of American Affluence. Random House.

Speer, E., Bhanji, J., & Delgado, M. (2014) Savoring the Past: Positive Memories Evoke Value Representations in the Striatum. Neuron, vol 84, issue 4, November 2014, p847-856

About the Author:

Andy has built a life for his family by working as a sales professional for many years and within multiple industries across the country. He has always had a tremendous love for teaching/coaching and also works as a professor in higher education and designates efforts as a performance coach. His primary vision is to help others achieve long lasting and succinct positive change, while helping them to create goals that are impactful yet pragmatic. Some theoretical foundations he utilizes and falls back on are from: Abraham Maslow, Martin Seligman and Fred Luthans.

@crackerjackprofessor

True learning involves way more than the ability to **memorize,**
It must focus on the impact and desire to **hypothesize!**

-Dr. Andy Swaithes

Made in the USA
Monee, IL
29 August 2022